A SEPHARDIC HOLOCA W9-DJL-887
FROM YUGOSLAVIA TO AN
INTERNMENT CAMP IN AMERICA

Sarinka

F. LINDA COHEN

I dedicate

this book to my parents, Shary Kabiljo z"l (of blessed memory) and Leon Kabiljo z"l, who instilled in me a profound love for my Jewish identity with their story of survival, their constant gratitude to God, and their quest for a better future. I can never thank them enough for their unconditional love and for their belief in me. From my mother's gentle soul, I learned kindness, and from my father's strong religious soul I learned to be proud of my Judaism and to stand up for what I believe is right and just, no matter what the majority thinks.

I also dedicate this book to my sister, Sylvia Simcha Kabiljo Rothschild, z"l (of blessed memory), one of the 23 babies born in the Emergency Refugee Shelter established at Fort Ontario, who unfortunately didn't live to see this book published. From my sweet sister I learned to help others by volunteering and to incorporate laughter and silliness into my life!

This book is also dedicated to all who perished in the Holocaust.

Testimonials

*S*arinka is beautifully written, historically accurate and a genuine page turner. Young people who read this book will understand the truth of being a refugee. They will learn what it means to lose everything—one's home, one's language, one's culture. And yet they will find hope in this very moving story." Ruth Gruber, March 14, 2010

> --Ruth Gruber (September 30, 1911 – November 17, 2016) was an award-winning Jewish American journalist, photographer, humanitarian, a United States government official, and author of nineteen books. She is the American heroine of this story.

*S*arinka is an evocative family memoir detailing the rarely heard Sephardic Jewish experience during the Shoah. What began as a daughter's hunger to faithfully recount as a family heirloom her parents' unique story of great love and great loss at the hands of the Nazis is now a gift to us all.

With fastidious attention to detail and to history, Linda Cohen immerses us in the twists, turns, terrors and daily miracles of her hastily wed parents' harrowing flight from their homes, their families, and eventually from their country. With painterly descriptions that engage all the senses, Cohen has us right there with Sarinka and Leon as the Nazis invade Yugoslavia mere hours before their planned wedding celebration, with the Muslim neighbors who came to their aid, with the partisans in the freezing woods, and with Ruth Gruber, the young American journalist who had a bold plan, capitalizing on Franklin Roosevelt's modest exception to tight US immigration quotas to help save a handful of Europe's doomed Jews.

Sarinka is a significant addition to Holocaust literature.

--Karen Tintori, author of Unto the Daughters: The Legacy of an Honor Killing in a Sicilian-American Family, St. Martins Press

Acknowledgements

I want to thank my husband, Dr. Ronald (Rick) Cohen, the love of my life who read and reread this story for me. Thank you to all three of my daughters Lauren, Jaime and Meredith, whose love, encouragement, and support propelled me to write this book. I also want to express gratitude to Sandy Gutman, Steven Katz, Leslie Martin, Karen Propis, Jeremy Rowe, Miles Stearn, Susan Terebelo, and my editor, Philip Turner—all who have helped in some way to see this to fruition. I must single out Karen Tintori Katz for pushing me and encouraging me to publish this book. Without her help and guidance, it might still be on my computer.

Thank you to Ruth Gruber, z"l (of blessed memory) who validated this story to the best of her ability, as she put forth precious time and effort to ensure accuracy in this book. I hope her family will appreciate the way she is portrayed as an America heroine.

I would also like to express my gratitude to Paul A. Lear, the Historic Site Manager of Fort Ontario who insisted I read a document written in 1946 by War Relocation Authority Refugee Program Officer Edward B Marks entitled *Token Shipment* and to Rebecca Fisher, Researcher at the Safe Haven Holocaust Refugee Shelter Museum who read and confirmed the accuracy of my parents' story to the best of her knowledge.

My sincere appreciation to Tammy Seidick for her cover design, Alexander Jishkariani, who created the map showing my parents' journey, as well as the family tree, and to Daria Lacy for her formatting expertise and publishing assistance.

Many heartfelt thanks to all of you.

F. Linda (Kabiljo) Cohen

Six million of our people live on in our hearts. We are their eyes that remember. We are their voice that cries out—The dreadful scenes that flow from their dead eyes to our open ones. And those scenes will be remembered exactly as they happened.

--Shimon Peres, z"l (of blessed memory) 1923-2016

I decided to devote my life to telling the story because I felt I owe something to the dead and anyone who doesn't remember betrays them again.

--Elie Wiesel, z"l (of blessed memory) 1928-2016

Introduction

For many years my father had what seemed like an impossible dream of reuniting with his sister and brother, his only surviving siblings. Almost thirty years had passed since he had last seen them. That dream finally came true when he saved enough for us to travel to Israel and Yugoslavia.

My father was young at heart. Laughter, jokes, gardening and dancing occupied his life when he wasn't working at any one of his multiple jobs or praying at the synagogue. He'd lost enough time due to the war. Life excited him and so did this trip.

My mother, eleven years younger, lived life cautiously— hesitant to try new things and although eager to go to Israel, she was reluctant to go back to the country that had taken everything away from her...the most heartfelt and irreplaceable of all, her mother and grandmother. Years after being in America and searching for answers she learned that after the war, there truly was nothing to go back to since her house was sold off and divided. "I'm afraid to see it now," she told me. "All I can think about is my mother and Nonna baking in our kitchen, and the wonderful memories that took place in our warm living room. My family's love and the contents of our house made it our home. It held keepsakes not only from my parents' lives, but also their parents and grandparents. I hate that all our family's treasures will never have their rightful place with us. Now, knowing the fate of our house in Travnik makes going back there after all these years even more difficult. I'll have to physically and emotionally face and feel the pain of losing my loved ones and our family's possessions all over again."

At times I would see her feeling depressed, remembering all she had lost, pushing herself to move forward and appreciate the blessings she now had. As we packed for this trip, I questioned her happiness here, in this country, but she reassured me she was happier in America than she ever was in Yugoslavia.

Now at the age of 18, for the first time in my life I had the privilege of meeting my only true relatives—my aunt Saphira in Israel and my uncle Isaac in Yugoslavia along with their families. After an amazing trip touring Jerusalem and Tel Aviv, we embraced these cities that touched our hearts and souls in so many ways—from watching my father finally reunite with his sister and meet his nephews for the first time to the connection we all felt to this amazing land of milk and honey we called our homeland. Sometimes I felt like I was walking through the history books and bible stories I read as a child. Our heritage came alive.

The week went too quickly and we were a little more skeptical about the second leg of this journey. My mother, not so anxious to return to her native country, forced herself to appear cheerful for my father's sake. She knew how important it was for him to reconnect with his brother after all these years. We had a short layover in Greece and then we boarded the plane for Yugoslavia. When we finally arrived at the Belgrade airport in June 1970, we were in line to go through customs and enter the country when we were singled out and asked to come with the authorities. My poor mother glanced at me with a fearful expression. My father was quickly speaking in fluent Serbian asking for some explanation as to what was happening. We were told there was an outbreak of cholera in Jerusalem and we would have to be vaccinated in order to enter the country. We were shocked and heard nothing of this outbreak. Needless to say, this was not a good beginning. Guided to a small room, we looked at each other with worry. Who knew what they were giving us? It was out of our hands and we were vaccinated on the spot. Only while researching this book did I discover that there was in fact an outbreak in an Arab village on the outskirts of Jerusalem that used sewage water to irrigate their vegetable crops thus creating the problem.

We finally boarded a train that took us to Sarajevo. Marveling at the countryside from the window, we all relaxed and my anticipation for this long-awaited reunion continued to build. I had no idea what to expect when we disembarked from the train.

The recognition was clear as they walked towards us. The two brothers looked so strikingly similar. Suddenly their pace quickened, and then they rushed to finally embrace, holding on for an unusually long time. I saw my father cry for the first time in my life. And then we all cried.

A few days into our visit, my uncle suggested we visit The Museum of Sarajevo, established in 1949, four years after World War II ended. We walked through the door and the stage was set for all that we would learn. As we strolled through, the story of Sarajevo's past came alive with a model of the Old Town, archeological collections and works of art, with the Jewish collection of utmost interest to us. My father came to an abrupt stop in front of a particularly large photo.

"Dad, what's wrong?" I asked.

"Oh, my God!"

My heart rate quickened. *What kind of "Oh my God" was that?*

"I can't believe it!" he continued.

I looked to my mother for some clue and saw her jaw drop. I couldn't imagine what evoked such a reaction in both of them.

My father finally said, "This is the picture that saved my life!"

It was the portrait of Rabbi Avraham Abinun, who I discovered was once a prominent rabbi of Travnik in 19th century Yugoslavia and later became known as the Grand Rabbi of Sarajevo from 1856 to 1858. The old man, with his traditional long beard and prominent religious kippah, died long before he would play a significant role in my family's history.

Many years later in 2007, I read an article in *Hadassah Magazine* about that very same building in Sarajevo, post-Yugoslavia. After reading it, my thoughts kept returning to the day I toured the museum with my parents. I contacted them to ask if my mother could have the picture returned to her after all these years. The curator told me that would be impossible because it was part of a permanent exhibit. However, they offered to send us a digital copy taken for preservation during the Bosnian-Croatian-Serbian War from 1991 to 1995. An email finally arrived with the following message from Zanka Karaman, Curator of the City Museum, Sarajevo:

"I hope the picture will revive some memories for your mother, not only painful, but pleasant ones too."

This was the best solution. The photograph would remain in the museum for many to view but we would have a smaller version mounted on canvas and hung in our home for my mother to enjoy.

I slowly peeled back the brown paper wrapping on January 22, 2008 to find the beautiful photo that now looked like an oil painting. Coming face to face with the photo mounted and framed, unexpectedly evoked tears that spilled down my cheeks. I fixated on the depth of his sad but wise eyes, nestled under thick, bushy eyebrows... eyes full of deep thoughts I only wished I knew. This miracle of my family's past was in my possession at last. If not for this picture, I would not be here to tell you this true story as it was told to me.

* * *

My parents revealed their story little by little when they thought I was old enough. It must not have been easy. Their words came haltingly as they shared bits and pieces over time. Their sighs and silences spoke volumes. As I asked repeatedly to hear the story, their details helped me visualize the inexplicable world from which they had emerged.

Sitting with my parents and having them relive their story as I questioned and listened was an unanticipated journey in itself. I realized how difficult it was to ask them to share this dark part of their lives and we often cried together. They were so proud of my attempt, however, to write their narrative memoir and insisted on continuing even at the most difficult times, so their experience could be documented.

I knew I had to share my parents' journey from Yugoslavia to America because too few knew of the impact that Ruth Gruber, an American heroine, had on the lives of 982 survivors in 1944 before World War II ended. Her actions, fortitude, and bravery saved my parents. Intent on trying to relate the most accurate account possible, I knew I couldn't write their story without researching and confirming what my parents shared. So, I investigated all that they revealed to verify everything I could, piecing together conversations from my parents, their friends, photos, videos, and historical information.

I hope you will hear my parents' voices as they recounted their story through me.

A copy of the photo of Rabbi Avraham Abinun: This picture played an integral part in my father's survival. It hung on the wall above my computer, looking down on me while I wrote this book. As strange as this may sound, there were times I felt as though he gave me the words to tell this story.

Part One

Sarinka

Chapter 1

Sunday, April 6, 1941
Travnik, Yugoslavia

Excitement overflowed in our usually quiet home. I woke up and listened to all the new and unfamiliar sounds that filled our house with relatives who had arrived on Friday, before Shabbat, when the Jewish day of rest began. Mama made her delicious *chicken paprikash* for Shabbat dinner that night, and the wedding weekend events began. Jewish law permits neither weddings nor travels from sundown Friday to sundown Saturday. Rest and chitchatting with one another filled the day after services Saturday morning. At sundown, however, the accordion came out and the festivities began. We sang, we ate, and we danced. All of the women gathered in a circle, hands around each other's waists, merrily bouncing about, light on our toes as we did the Yugoslav *kolo*. My heart overflowed with happiness. I scanned the room full of smiles, listened to the laughter and recognized this pure feeling of joy.

Leon celebrated with his own family. With his siblings in town for the wedding, they surely drank shots of *slivovitz,* a plum brandy made locally, and they too danced and sang until late into the night.

On Sunday morning, the day of our wedding, the aroma of *pastel,* awakened and energized my senses. Mama prepared the savory meat pie for our lunch before the ceremony later that afternoon. As my eyes opened, I focused on the exquisite ivory wedding dress adorned with pearls and lace that hung on the closet door with the veil and blusher so carefully selected. *Everything is ready for today.*

Suddenly I heard a roaring, a roaring that shook the whole house… sounds of planes flying over…more like an invasion of planes. It sent a shiver down my entire body. *No negative thoughts*, I told myself. *This is my wedding day, the day I've waited for my whole life.* Despite the scary feelings I felt deep down I forced myself to let go of this negativity that so often loomed over me. *Maybe it's just some kind of army exercise,* I convinced myself.

Once the frightening sounds had stopped, I spent a few more moments in quiet reflection, then leapt out of bed to enjoy my last breakfast at home with my mother before anyone else awoke. I grabbed my robe and practically danced into the kitchen smiling from ear to ear until I saw my mother's worried face. My whole demeanor changed.

"You heard the planes too? What do you think it means?" I asked.

"Of course I heard them," my mother answered. Then, trying to sound cheerful, she added, "But don't worry about anything today. Today you're getting married!" With those simple words she put my mind at ease as only a mother could. Although I still wasn't totally persuaded, this was too special a day to ruin with needless worry.

We drank Turkish coffee from my mother's beautiful demitasse cups, saved for special occasions, and she prepared her scrumptious *burek*— my favorite cheese-filled pastry, with poppy seed cakes and her special chocolate hazelnut torte for dessert. The wedding would not be until late afternoon, so we had time to relax.

I never expected this to be such a bittersweet moment—thrilled to become Leon's wife, but sad to leave Mama alone. As we shared this intimate time together my mother tenderly said, "Sarinka, how is it possible that today you will become a married woman? You will go with your husband and begin a new life together." She stopped and I noticed her tears. "Perhaps one day soon I will even become a *Nonna*! Tata would have been so happy if he lived to see this day."

"I thought about him this morning too, Mama, wishing so much he could share this simcha, this joy, with us. Tata would have been so proud and excited to walk me down the aisle. He's always in my heart, but today, even more so. I can just see his joyous face!" I responded as my own tears welled up, and my mother embraced me.

I went to my bedroom to continue packing. Following the wedding and a short honeymoon, Leon and I would move immediately to Tuzla, a town about 55 miles away, where he lived and worked. The doorbell rang and the voice I heard speaking to my mother sounded like Leon's but with a frantic tone. *It couldn't be him...he knew we weren't supposed to see each other until the wedding.*

I heard a knock at my bedroom door and when I opened it I was shocked to see Leon standing there. "Couldn't wait to see me until this afternoon?" I said opening the door with a big smile. But seeing his expression, I realized something was very wrong.

"Sarinka, didn't you hear the news?" he asked.

"What news? Is someone not coming?" The wedding was the only thing on my mind.

"No one will come. The Germans invaded Yugoslavia this morning. I heard it on the radio."

"Oh my God! The planes I heard...this can't be happening!" I felt like someone had punched me in the stomach. I slowly sat down on the edge of my bed. " What does this mean?"

"It's too dangerous for anyone to come. We must go to the rabbi and see if he will marry us immediately."

"I can't even think. Please tell me this is just a nightmare," I said.

"I wish I could. I know how you have been looking forward to this day, as I have, but we have to think fast. Please, let's go to the rabbi now and ask if he can marry us this morning. We'll get married and then go back to Tuzla. As far as we know the Nazis aren't there yet. At least I've got my job."

I sat paralyzed, weeping with disappointment and fear. My mother heard me crying and ran into the room. Gasping as I tried to speak, I told her what had happened.

"Leon, what do you think you should do?" Mama asked.

"I think we need to go the rabbi as soon as possible and see what he thinks," Leon told her.

"Mama, what should we do?"

"Leon›s right. Go now."

Wiping my tears, I tried to pull myself together. With Leon's arm around me, we briskly walked, trying to be vigilant since we had no idea what was really going on at this point in Travnik. When we arrived, Leon explained everything to the rabbi. In a soft-spoken serious tone, he said he would come to my house to marry us.

As the news spread, pandemonium exploded. All those who'd arrived early panicked and packed to leave as quickly as possible, worried about children they had left with friends or relatives. Leon felt so sad when his sister left by 10 a.m. hoping she could at least be at the hurried ceremony.

. I knew the rabbi would be at my house soon. There was no time to even think of donning the beautiful wedding gown I had selected for the most special day of my life, but instead I wore a simple lace dress. I would wear my veil during the ceremony, if nothing else. I had spoken to the rabbi earlier when we met about the wedding as to why it was a Jewish custom for a bride to wear a veil. I knew the common explanation of the groom lifting it to see the bride's face before the wedding to be sure he was marrying the correct sister—based on our patriarch Jacob who was tricked into marrying Leah, Rachel's older sister—but in this case I had no sisters. I was curious if this was the only reason. What the rabbi explained touched me deeply. He told me that by covering my face, the *chatan* (bridegroom) was reaffirming that although the *kallah* (bride) may look beautiful on this day, his love for her is not about her outer beauty but more about the kallah's character and views of life. He said the chatan could cover the kallah's sweet face and still marry her because this is just one level of her true beauty. At the very least, I wanted to have the memory of Leon seeing me with my veil.

Feeling numb as I waited for the rabbi to arrive, I glanced around the living room—the room that no longer held a single guest. I looked at the boxes of all sizes that filled the parlor, wrapped in decorative wedding paper, adorned with ribbons, presents carefully chosen with love. I imagined the synagogue, as it should have been. I pictured the exquisite room where my wedding was supposed to have taken place at four o'clock that day. I imagined us standing under the beautiful white chuppa, a wedding canopy with beautiful foliage wrapped around the four poles. Lost in the reverie of what should have been, I faintly heard Leon calling me back to reality. "He's here," he said tenderly.

The rabbi arrived at 10:00 a.m. and we were hastily married under the portable chuppa he brought with him. Everything was so rushed and upsetting. I don't even remember who held the *chuppa* over our heads at this pivotal moment in our lives when Leon and I said our sacred vows. Then, before the breaking of the glass which is how our wedding tradition concludes, the rabbi reminded us this was not only done to remember the destruction of the Temple in Jerusalem over two thousand years ago, but there is another reason. His look penetrated us as he said, "You would normally be at the pinnacle of happiness, but this is a dangerous time. Breaking the glass must also remind you of your commitment to each other in the future even when times ahead may get very rough. Relationships are fragile too, so treat your marriage with special care. But always remember, just as shards of glass are plentiful, this represents hope for the future too—for plenty of happiness in life and hopefully children."

I know the wise rabbi wanted to end on a positive happy note. I tried to take it all in and be hopeful, but even he could not suppress my fears.

This was not the way my wedding day was supposed to be.
Family and friends now gone.
Not one gift ever opened.

Instead of all the happiness, we were left only with fear of what tomorrow would bring.

Sarinka Montiljo and Leon Kabiljo married April 6, 1941

Flora and Morić Montiljo

Sarinka and her parents

Chapter 2

1931-1932
Travnik, Yugoslavia

Growing up as the only child of Flora (Bukića, her nickname) and Morić Montiljo, most would agree I led a relatively easy life. I attended a good school, had servants who catered to me, and had Jewish, as well as Catholic and Muslim friends—all different religions but we all got along. It was a special community. My family was rather well off, and may have been the envy of others in our small town. But as life would have it, that too would change.

Our home was in a small town in the Lašva river valley at the base of Mount Vlasic in Bosnia. One summer evening, I gazed from my window at the beautiful surrounding mountain. Tears blurred my vision. Our housekeeper, Katçiaćia, repeatedly called me for dinner, but I had no appetite.

When Mama arrived home late that night, I heard laughter as she said goodnight to her latest suitor. How could she dress in her finest and dine out almost every evening? Still young and beautiful, she had moved on with her life after Tata died. I knew it didn't mean she loved him any less, but even though it had been many months and her thirty-day mourning period was technically over, her behavior was unacceptable to me. Nothing seemed to assuage my grief.

I loved Tata so much and often cried myself to sleep thinking of him. At thirty-eight, he had died before his time and thirteen was too young to lose him. He spent many nights with me in the kitchen as he helped me memorize my multiplication tables. I hated the rote drills but loved our time together. When we walked to the synagogue he listened to my chatter with the same focus he gave his customers.

My father, Morić Montiljo was a hardworking, prominent citizen in our town, respected by everyone in Travnik, Yugoslavia. He owned a liquor store that provided us with more than a comfortable life in our large home, complete with servants. We lived above the store at Two Obale Lašva, so he was always close by.

A religious man, he went to the only synagogue in Travnik every Saturday and eventually became the president of the small congregation. Although the women sat in the balcony, separate from the men, the rabbi of the synagogue allowed me, as a young girl, to sit on the main floor next to my father. I took note of Tata's kindness to the men, including the most deprived in our village. Tata smiled and spoke softly and gently to everyone, rich and poor alike. He anonymously provided funds for meals on Shabbat to help others "not as fortunate as us," he told me. From Friday at sunset to the following evening after nightfall, Tata refrained from work. Instead he fed his spiritual soul as we are instructed to do on Shabbat. He also founded a small Jewish graveyard for the congregants. By the time I turned twelve, he had already shown me by his example how to live life.

I noticed Tata didn't have the energy he always had for me and the doctor seemed to be a frequent visitor. Information wasn't readily shared with a young adolescent, but I tried to listen to my parents' whispers.

For ten months my sadness swelled as I watched Tata's health deteriorate. He tired easily and struggled to continue working. After a tough day at work his legs looked red and inflamed. One day the doctor arrived with leeches in a container. Leech therapy was supposed to help my father with his blood circulation. The thought of the doctor putting leeches on his legs made me nauseous and told me things weren't getting any better. Some time after, I overheard the doctor tell my mother his high blood pressure insidiously led to serious kidney damage. I didn't understand any of this.

After school one day, I came home, hung up my jacket and set my books down on the table. *Why were my father's keys here? Strange that he would be home so early.* I ran to his bedroom to give him a big hug, eagerly shouting, "Tata!"

My mother ran after me, putting both hands on my shoulders to stop me from bursting in. "Sarinka," she said, "Tata left work early because he feels ill. It's his kidneys again. Go into the room quietly and speak softly to him."

Heavy-hearted, I quietly entered the room. I spoke softly. "Tata, the teacher called on me today and you will be proud to know I answered all the multiplication answers correctly!"

Weak and tired, Tata managed to say the words I loved to hear, "Sarinka, you're incredible."

I had no idea this would be the last time my father would say those precious words to me. He managed a faint smile, encouraging me to tell him more about my day and my plans with friends. I held his hand and tried my best to cheer him. I glanced at the prayer book he kept by his bed, smaller than even his billfold. *Would he ever pray from this special little book again?*

Later that evening, my mother sat down next to me. "Sarinka, I wrote to your uncles and told them how sick Tata is. They are traveling home from Italy to help us with the business."

This news instantly told me the prognosis for my father was very grim. There could be no other explanation for Yaakov and even Davo, the youngest and an accomplished dentist, who never liked practicing dentistry, to leave the community where they now lived and worked. The mere fact that Yaakov was bringing his wife Sarina and their two sons was a grave sign.

"You don't think Tata will live, do you? Please be honest with me. I am not a little girl anymore, Mama."

"Of course, I will always have hope, Sarinka. But I am trying to face the future…just in case," Mama said, trying her best to hold back tears. "Tata built this successful store from nothing and we can't let him down and neglect it. He wouldn't want us to do that, right?"

"I guess so," I responded sadly. Of course she was right.

One day, I kissed Tata before I left for school, but he could not even speak. It had been a week since he last spoke to me. Each day, I rushed home looking for improvement, but each day he was worse. Eventually, I lost my smile. I began to accept that my prayers would go unanswered.

Just eight days after he came home early from work, I lost my father. My mother held me as we sobbed by the window watching the men carry Tata's body out of our house and onto a wagon. It was a custom that women were prohibited from attending the funeral. Without a word, we comforted each other the only way we knew how, by crying together, heavy sighs separating the breaths of air that kept us from suffocating in our sorrow.

Soon after, the rabbi came to us for the rending of our garments. He asked us to recite the blessing after him as he murmured the words, "*Baruch atah Adonai E-loi-hei-nu melech haolam, dayan ha'emet.* Blessed are you, Lord our God, Ruler of the universe, the true Judge." Then, as our laws instruct us, we made a tear in our blouses close to our hearts, a physical sign showing our community we were the bereaved family of the deceased. The rabbi explained this ancient custom of tearing our clothes is an expression of pain and sorrow over the death of a loved one.

He spoke softly. "When your mourning period is over, mend the tear, as you will need to mend your hearts. The mending will help heal, but the scar will remind you of the removal of this precious person from your lives. Your family cloth, no longer whole, joins all who have suffered tragedy." The rabbi's words touched my soul.

How ironic—Morić Montiljo was the first man buried in the small Jewish graveyard he had founded. Even though I wasn't physically present, a piece of my heart and soul went deep into the earth with him, and my life would never be the same. My mother made sure to mark it with a beautiful stone.

I wandered the house with an emptiness I couldn't shake, unable to find any comfort. On our piano I spotted a photo of my parents and me celebrating my tenth birthday. We were on our outside porch. Mama and Tata embraced me as I smiled holding my newest doll. What a special memory. I clutched the frame to my heart, sobbing, longing to take one more special walk with him, to hear the sound of his voice, but most of all, wishing for one more hug and kiss to hold me the rest of my life. It was too difficult to grasp the finality of his death.

Shiva, our seven-day mourning period began. As our custom dictates, Mama and I sat on pillows low to the floor, surrounded by my father's brothers and sisters, who were also sitting Shiva throughout the week. Nonna, Mama's mother who had lived with us ever since I could remember, grieved the loss of my father but in the Jewish religion a mother-in-law is not required to sit Shiva. Instead she worked hard to console us, catering to our every need.

Neighbors and relatives poured into our house with meals and sweets to comfort us. About seventy Jewish families lived in Travnik at that time. Our house bulged with our Jewish, Catholic, and Muslim friends who came to pay their respects. I greeted everyone stoically, hoping to make Tata proud, but merely going through the motions. On the seventh day, after all the visitors left, we peacefully divided his belongings among the family. My mother inherited all the wealth he accrued from his successful store and since she continued to manage it our current life style continued.

When the week was over, I could almost taste the void that filled the house, like bitter herbs constantly floating around me. I imagined Tata and Mama sitting on the needlepoint-covered chairs while she poured Turkish coffee into delicate demitasse cups from a little brass coffee pot we called a *džezva*. I pictured their guests sitting on our plush rosy sofa selecting from Mama's delicious homemade sweet cakes, everyone talking and laughing. The polished mahogany baby grand piano my father bought for me sat by the window on a needlepointed rug hugging the polished parquet floors. Beautiful art adorned our walls. Mama had decorated our home so tastefully, but who would enjoy it all now? How could we go on without Tata?

Nothing excited me. I lingered in bed and skipped meals. I never called my friends and in time they stopped calling me. Mama and Nonna searched for ways to lift my spirits. Together they made my favorite Sephardic dishes. Mama prepared Palačinka, thin crepe-like pancakes filled with raspberry jam, rolled up, and sprinkled with powdered sugar. Nonna prepared *pastel* because she knew I couldn't turn it down. She fried sweet onions, browned and seasoned ground beef, and then scooped it in between two layers of thin dough that Mama prepared and baked until crisp. Neighbors walking by delighted in the aroma that wafted from our open kitchen window. For dessert, they baked their specialties and my favorites, *baklava* and strudel made with homemade phyllo dough filled with chopped apples and nuts. I watched as Nonna brushed each sheet with melted sweet butter, filled it with an apple walnut mixture, and then drenched it with syrup made from water, sugar, and fresh lemon. It was hard to resist when they teamed up like this. The smell alone could lure anyone into their kitchen, but even with their best efforts my appetite was barely aroused.

As the weeks passed, we longed for the way Tata prepared for Friday night. After he closed the store, he would shower, shave, and don his best clothes for Shabbat. Now, Mama, Nonna, and I welcomed in Shabbat on our own. We lit the Shabbat candles, covered our eyes, and waved our hands three times in a circular motion around them, repeating the blessing in a sacred way that made ordinary candles holy. Mama sang the blessing through her tears as she tried her hardest to assume his role. But without Tata there to lead the prayers over the wine and challah before dinner, and without him placing his hands on my head to recite the Shabbat blessing for the daughters over me, followed by a kiss on my head, Friday nights suddenly felt like salt on a raw, open wound.

We gathered with my mother's sister Lunchka for the holidays. As Sephardic Jews with ancestors who were expelled from Spain in 1492, we celebrated holidays a little differently than most Eastern European Ashkenazi Jews. On *Tu B'Shevat*, a festive holiday celebrating the planting of trees, we went to Aunt Lunchka's house, who also lived in Travnik, to decorate containers and fill them with as many different fruits and nuts as we could. On Purim we gave our friends and family baskets filled with goodies, believing that the more gifts we gave, the more we would receive spiritually. Mama and Nonna insisted that time spent preparing the packages would help console me, but with the most essential ingredient missing from all the holidays, my normal life couldn't resume. There was no normal anymore.

Mama pushed me to return to my studies, but my mind was elsewhere. Still numb and hollow inside, my feelings of loneliness grew. I clung to my precious memories, but having no brothers or sisters to share my grief made it even more difficult. I could not even think about returning to school, though I knew my mother would insist. I struggled to adjust to my life without my beloved father.

Tata died and life as I knew it was over at the tender age of twelve. My relationship with my mother took a toll. Now she made me furious.

Sarinka at Catholic School
(First row of students behind
the teacher, first on the left.)

Chapter 3

Irarely left our house except to go to school. Earlier in my childhood, my parents sent me to Hebrew school but after constant protesting that they were too strict, my mother unfortunately let me quit. For general studies, they decided on a Catholic Jesuit school, as other Jewish parents in Travnik had. They chose this path because they wanted the best education possible for me and we didn't have a Jewish day school in our town. Jesuit schools offered a more academically challenging curriculum than the public school.

After the Shiva period ended, I couldn't put off returning to my studies any longer. At the awkward age of twelve, with my unruly thick caramel-colored curly hair, I reluctantly dressed in the school uniform I detested. Skinnier from all my sadness, I donned my white-collared, buttoned down long sleeved black dress that covered my knees and hung on me.

Now, more than ever, I felt out of place there. My mind wandered during the morning prayers that meant nothing to me. Core subjects challenged me. The nuns were demanding, and as a struggling student I felt their wrath, instead of their understanding.

Fortunately, I had two best friends, Vera and Mućika. They helped me get through high school, but as teenagers we also got into our share of trouble. In class one day, Vera and Mućika were smiling during a time when all should have been paying close attention to a particularly complicated lesson. I should have known better than to glimpse at either of them, but Vera looked at me with her contagious grin. My math teacher glanced up with a stare that went right through me and that was it. I tried to keep it to a smile, pushing it down, struggling to suppress the urge to burst out laughing. The last thing I wanted was to draw attention to myself, but the harder I tried, the harder it was to keep my composure. Finally, I lost control and exploded with laughter. The whole class turned to look at me.

With a pointer in her hand, the nun moved slowly toward me. As she approached, I continued laughing uncontrollably. When she reached my desk, her pointer rapped it with such fury I thought it would break in half. She yelled, "Sarinka, please…share with all of us what you think is so funny."

I wanted to run out of the room, but I froze right where I sat. My laughter was swallowed by fear. Sister Judith leaned toward me and grabbed my hair. She pulled me toward the piano and pushed me under it as if I was a rag doll. Everyone stared. I felt heat slither up to my face, which blushed crimson, bringing even more attention to myself.

"Now, stay there until you are ready to attend to this lesson. How dare you laugh while I am trying to teach you? You, of all students! You, who needs it the most! No wonder you are doing so poorly. Your mind is far from your studies. Your mother will hear about this."

Mama recognized how I struggled—even more so now—and tried to remedy the situation by spoiling me. With nothing expected of me, I never helped around the house or learned how to cook. Our servants, Katçia, Hasia, and Boshya, did those things.

Knowing Tata felt strongly about my private piano lessons, I continued them for his sake. Mrs. Lubić was a *zaftig* woman with dark finger-waved hair who rarely smiled. The long dark dress that buttoned up to her neck complemented her crankiness. She constantly complained that I didn't practice enough. Perhaps she was right and I should have pushed myself more. After mastering *Beethoven's Minuet in G* and then the even more challenging, *Fur Elise* —my favorite piece out of everything she taught me—she saw my potential. She urged me to learn theory and play classical compositions, but my preference for popular tunes persisted. Mrs. Lubić found me to be her most frustrating student in the seven years she taught me.

I managed to graduate from high school and then, like many girls, attended a trade school. For me this meant learning to be a seamstress. Frequently I heard, "Sarinka, are you working on your dress?"

"No, Mama."

"How will you finish in time? You need to learn to do something if you don't want to work in our store."

"I don't like it. I don't have the patience to sit and sew. I'd rather be out with my friends or drawing, or even playing piano! Anything would be better!"

Mama noticed that I often doodled and drew. One day she surprised me with a watercolor set and I began painting. Soon, scenes of mountains, sea sides, autumn trees, birds, and portraits of people filled my room. I read, painted, practiced piano, and spent leisure time with my friends, but now at the age of 18, I knew the time had come for me to do something more productive.

More schooling was not an option I would consider, and change in general made me anxious. So, with Mama's encouragement I finally decided to work at our liquor store and was happy not to venture out to a different place for employment. It gave me solace to work in the store with my mother, and my uncle who stayed on to help us. Although many years had passed since my father's death, his spiritual presence there still soothed me.

Luckily, each summer mama encouraged me to take the train to Makarska, a small resort town by the Adriatic Sea where our family friend,

Mazalta Katan, owned a charming gift shop filled with souvenirs from the coast. I could hardly wait for this annual visit. My excitement grew when the pomegranate colored roofs of the homes that embraced the coast came into view.

As soon as we arrived, I ran to catch a glimpse of the sparkling sea with fresh eyes, feeling comforted by the far off horizon. I slowly inhaled, savoring my first breath of the salty air. The waves rolled in and grabbed each grain of sand leaving only a veil of lace across the beach, reminding me of Nonna's white lace tablecloth as it billowed across the Shabbat table. The sea consoled me, as did the sound of families laughing and playing in the water. I smiled wistfully.

Spending fun-filled days at this seaside resort with my friends made for great summers. We played ball and laughed over the silliest things. The beautiful scenery fed my artistic soul and encouraged me to paint. In the evenings we dined at cafés by the water as we listened to lively music. Then we walked and as the music from one café grew distant we began to hear a lively accordion playing at the next one. It seemed like there was always music in the air. We gazed at the fashionable outfits the wealthy women wore as they strolled the promenade each evening. It was such a happy time during the day, yet at bedtime, an empty feeling prevailed. Makarska was merely a bandage that eased my loneliness.

I had no idea of the foreboding twists and turns life had in store for me.

I had no idea this was my last visit to the Adriatic seaside.

Chapter 4

1940

After a warm welcome back, complete with all the foods I loved most, Mama (who probably thought about this all summer) sweetly began the conversation. "Sarinka, it's time we start looking for a husband for you. I have been quiet until now but perhaps we need to start actively pursuing this. Nonna agrees with me. Surely you're eager to see your friends at the Jewish Club after being away. How about dressing up and strolling the promenade in town before heading over there? It wouldn't hurt to push yourself a bit."

"Oh Mama…I'm only 22. I'll find someone in my own time." But, she wouldn't take no for an answer. Like a debutante, I now carefully selected each outfit, wearing the latest styles and finest accessories, to enhance my highly encouraged search for a husband.

One evening we were all at the Jewish club having a wonderful time, talking, laughing and dancing to radio music when a crash of broken glass stunned us all. "What was that?" It sounded like Mućika screamed. My eyes searched desperately. When I found my best friend I could see blood dripping from her arm. Someone yelled. "Run! Run! It's the *Ustaša!*" The feared *Ustaša* who were members of the Croatian Revolutionary Movement, frequently harassed the Jews in town. They had thrown chunks of hard coal at the club's windows! Everyone rushed for the door, screaming. Mućika and I ran to her house crying, not looking back. She was not badly injured but we were both shaken up. As her mother bandaged the cut, she told us she heard rumblings about things like this happening, but none of us had ever experienced anything firsthand.

Although the Nazis were not yet in Yugoslavia their venom had started to spread as the *Ustaša* embraced the indoctrination of the German soldiers. We became more vigilant as the times changed around us, avoiding any evidence of being Jewish. No one wanted to become the target of the *Ustaša's* violent acts. We went through everything in our homes, hiding religious objects of any kind in case any *Ustaša* came to our house. The photo of a rabbi that hung in our hallway ever since I could remember now hid in our attic along with our other Judaic items and books. Even Nonna's Shabbat candlesticks that we used every Friday night were now out of sight.

Our daily lives continued as normal as possible. We continued working in the store, but I stayed in more, all of us increasingly nervous now. One day, my mother asked, " How would you like to visit your aunt in Bijeljina? She tells me things are still calm there."

"I'd love that! Isn't it far though? Hours from here?"

"Well, it would mean staying overnight along the way to make the necessary train connection and it would be inappropriate for a young single girl to stay in a guesthouse by herself. I'll see what I can do."

Mama went to the post office where she telephoned a distant relative, Simha Kabiljo, in the small town of Žepče. She asked if I could spend one night to alleviate her fears of me traveling alone and to make the connection I needed. Simha was pleased to have me and assured my mother that someone would meet me at the station and escort me to her house.

With everything planned, I began packing, thrilled to escape the monotonous life in Travnik where everyone, including my friends appeared tense and anxious. I also felt scared and nervous, but I needed to go. Mama and Nonna came to the train station to send me off with big hugs.

Mama warned, "Don't stare at anyone. Just keep to yourself and mind your own business. Don't venture off either on your way to Bijeljina or home. These are dangerous times and you know we will worry. Please remember to write as soon as you can."

"Mama, Nonna, I'll be fine and back before you know it. I'll be safer there. You said yourself they haven't had the trouble we're having here. Please, please don't worry about me. Thank you so much for making all the arrangements. With those words, I gave them each an enormous hug and a kiss goodbye, climbed aboard the train, and waved as the train pulled away.

I stared out the window at the beautiful countryside for a long time, thinking back to our conversation. *Maybe Mama was right.* At the age of twenty-two, I dated, but no one seriously. Many of my friends had already married. I knew all the young men in my town and didn't see a potential husband among them. No butchers or morticians for me. I wanted a husband to have clean hands! I decided I simply hadn't met my *bashert*, the one destined for me. I needed patience, something I often lacked. I dozed, read and stared out the window until I reached Žepče.

As the train pulled to a stop, I gingerly stepped down, and looked around. Confidently dressed in my favorite lapis suit and ivory heels, I surveyed the station for someone hopefully looking for me. I noticed a striking, distinguished man in an official government uniform, looking fit and dapper. He looked far too young to have his slightly balding silver hair, but along with his handsomely carved facial features, this made him look even more noteworthy. My heart throbbed as this gentleman approached. Fixated on his beautiful green eyes I heard him say, *"Dobro veče.* Excuse me. Are you Sarinka?"

"Yes. Did Simha send you?" I answered, wondering if he sensed my jittery nerves.

"I'm sorry. I should have introduced myself. I'm her son, Leon, and I just arrived from Tuzla to visit my mother. She asked me to meet you. Let me take you to my mother's house so you can get settled. Then, if you would like, we can go to a café. You must be hungry."

"I'd love that," I responded with an innocent but flirtatious smile.

Leon looked so handsome in his government uniform. He was kind, polite, funny, and so full of life! We talked, laughed, and drank wine as we dined at an outdoor café and enjoyed the lovely evening before we went back to his mother's house for my one night stay. I could hardly sleep.

The next morning I thought I noticed a twinkle in Leon's eyes and wondered if he shared my excitement. Did he yearn for more time together as I did? After breakfast, I reluctantly packed my bags. Leon would at least walk me back to the station.

"Before you leave, can I have your address?" he asked.

"Of course, but you must give me yours as well," I responded. My hand trembled with excitement as I wrote it down for him. *"Dovidjenja,* Leon."

Leon Kabiljo 1934, 26 years old, six years before he met Sarinka.

"Dovidjenja, Sarinka," he replied, and sent me off with a peck on each check. "Be safe."

Was that just a courtesy kiss? I didn't want to make too much of it. We hardly knew each other. In Travnik that would only happen if you were good friends or out on date, hoping it turned into more. The thought of his lips touching my skin sent a shiver down me. That little kiss embraced my whole being and I found myself reliving that moment over and over.

I looked forward to this month-long visit with my aunt. We enjoyed quality time with each other and although my time was also filled with many social gatherings, it seemed like a long four weeks.

I went to bed each night thinking of Leon, sometimes my thoughts even woke me up in the middle of the night, and he was my first thought when I opened my eyes—so unusual for me. No one I had ever gone out with had this affect on me.

I had already written a note to Simha thanking her for her hospitality. After much thought, I decided to write Leon a note as well. I thanked him for such a delightful evening and told him how much I enjoyed the laughter and conversation. Later, I learned that Leon had shown my note to his older brother Isaac, who encouraged him to write back. Isaac told him that at thirty-three with a secure government job for the Internal Revenue Service he too should think about getting married.

I prayed I'd see him again during my one-night stopover on the way home to Travnik.

Taking great pains to look my best, I stepped off the train and found Simha there to greet me. *"Dobro veče*, Sarinka. *Kako ste?"*

"Fine thank you, and you?"

"Dobro sam."

" Glad to hear that. I am surprised to see you and not Leon here."

"Ah, Sarinka! Did you forget Leon works in Tuzla and only comes home from time to time?" Simha looked at me grinning, seeing through my phony smile, hardly able to hide my disappointment.

Shortly after I returned home, a letter from Leon arrived.

Dear Sarinka,

I was so happy to hear from you, and I was wondering if I could see you again. This time, I will come to you. Please let

*me know. As an accountant, I work for the government as an
Internal Revenue tax collector in Tuzla, so I will have to arrange for the days off.*

Anxiously waiting your reply,

Leon

A picture of the Travnik market place that Leon and
Sarinka (Shary) displayed in their home.

Leon traveled a few hours by train to visit me. He stayed at a nearby
boarding house and we saw each other every day for a week. As fall slowly introduced itself, the beautiful foliage accompanied us on our long
walks. We strode along the busy open bazaar shops stopping to look at all
the fresh fruits and vegetables, open burlap bags of rice, salt, flour, along
with freshly baked breads and pies proudly displayed. Leon insisted on
having me select a pie to bring home to Mama and Nonna, a gesture they
would surely love. I took him to the stall where my family bought our

special cozy "Yugoslav" slippers—a dark maroon woolen design knitted up to the ankle like socks, but sewn to leather bottoms.

"I think I'll buy a pair. It will be my souvenir of this visit," he said.

"Let me show you the fine handmade leather slippers like my father used to wear. You would enjoy these much more. Who knows? Perhaps a gift could be in your future," I said with a grin.

We chatted for hours about everything and anything. It didn't matter what the topic.

"Leon, tell me more about your life."

"I grew up on a small farm. It's been a tough life for my mother. My father, a businessman in Vienna, died from bone cancer when I was only six years old. My mother was pregnant with my youngest sister so none of us were able to attend his funeral. It was so sad. It was up to her to keep our farm going in order to feed my eight siblings and me. We never had much. Somehow we survived though. Then my beautiful sister, Sarika got very sick and passed away—just nineteen years old. I worked for the government in Novi Sad at that time and I didn't make it in time for the funeral. There are no words for how I felt. I tried to comfort my mother. It was so heartbreaking, but she refused to give in to her sorrow. She's a religious woman and her faith helped her get through it all. Everyone in our town loves her. She helps all those in need because she's knowledgeable in herbal medicine and takes plants and herbs to people who are sick in her small community. She even suggests what they need to eat and drink to feel better. A few years ago I was quite sick and my mother took care of me too. I am probably the closest to her...and now I'm the youngest. My brothers requested I move closer to home which I is why I took a job in Tuzla. They all had businesses so they couldn't pick up and move as easily as I could. I try my best to take care of her because she's so busy taking care of everyone else."

"Our lives are so different. I grew up with servants, never having to worry about my next meal. When I was a little girl, my father purchased an insurance policy that will come due when I marry. Even after my father died money wasn't an issue because my mother and uncles worked hard to keep the liquor store going. I didn't have the hard life you did, but I always felt very lonely as an only child."

Leon continued, "I hope to marry and be able to support my family one day, like your father. That's why I made sure I went to school to learn accounting. For ten years I have had a secure government job. All my brothers followed my father's footsteps and had businesses, but I wanted to go to school and get an education. I completed high school and business college to become an accountant, since I am good with numbers. That's why it was easiest for me to relocate to be close enough to look after my mother."

As we tried to get to know each other, we had a lot of these discussions. I realized that being with him made me happy and for the first time since my father died, I laughed from my heart. It surprised me how comfortable I felt with him.

Before the weather turned too cold, I wanted to take Leon to a treasured spot near the base of the mountains where I often picnicked with my parents when I was a child. I spread out a blanket and began to unpack the dinner Mama and Nonna helped me cook, a meal I took an unusual interest in preparing. We shared a special bottle of wine as we ate *pastel, ćevapčići* (small grilled logs of seasoned ground beef and lamb), rice stuffed vegetables, and baklava for dessert. My mother and Nonna knew the way to a man's heart and had insisted on this menu.

After he left, we continued to write letters over the next couple of months. More visits followed. My mother raised her eyebrows and smiled as she observed my cheerfulness and a spring in my step. In fact, she said that I had become strangely agreeable as I hummed and sang absent-mindedly around the house.

Whenever Leon wrote to tell me he was coming for another visit, I counted the days. I planned what outfit to wear when I greeted him, what foods to prepare, and new things we could do together.

Now with winter approaching, the days were shorter. Immediately after Leon's arrival, I asked if he wanted to take a stroll so we could have some cherished time alone. I chattered away and Leon listened, more quietly than usual. When I finally took a breath, Leon spoke.

"Sarinka, I know we have only been seeing each other for three months, but I love spending time with you and I think about you constantly. I realize I'm eleven years older than you, but that just makes me more responsible and ready to settle down. I can't bear the thought of leaving you after each visit, and hate when we're apart. I worry about you with the *Ustaša's* presence more prevalent here. Sarinka, I love you. You might say it's too soon to say that, but I know it in my heart. I want to ask you something and I hope you won't be shocked. ...Will you marry me?"

Oh, my God! I can't believe I'm hearing this! " Yes! Yes! Yes!" I replied as tears of joy filled my eyes. No other words needed to be said. I melted in his arms as we embraced, and he kissed me passionately. I knew without a doubt I wanted to spend the rest of my life with him.

Both families approved of the match. In those days, it was common for distant relatives to wed because marrying within our religion was paramount. My great-grandmother and Leon's grandmother were sisters. Had I not gone to visit my great aunt in a distant town and needed a place to stay along the way, our paths might not have crossed.

We decided to get married on Sunday, April 6th and I wanted to shout it from the rooftops. I wished I could have shared the news with my father, who would have been so thrilled for me. Finally, I went out on my porch and shouted, "Tata, I'm getting married! I need your blessing, too!"

Part Two

Leon

Chapter 5

April 7, 1941—The day after we were hastily married.

I imagined my beautiful bride as she would have been had we been able to have the wedding we planned. I'll never see Sarinka in the beautiful ivory bridal dress she had selected for this special day. Nothing was the way it was supposed to be. Our suitcases were packed before the wedding day, but our honeymoon plans for Bled, a Slovenian resort town in the foothills of the Julian Alps, became only a dream. Watching Sarinka's excitement about this trip gave me such pleasure, but now fear drove our journey together down a very different road. I worried how she would cope with our new unknown circumstances, especially since she had led such a protected life.

After we heard about the invasion everyone from our extended families quickly returned to their hometowns, not knowing what to expect. Terror and tension could be felt everywhere around us. Everything about this was wrong.

We sat and waited at Sarinka's house for two days, not knowing what to do. Finally, I insisted we go back to Tuzla, where I hoped we would be safe. Since I had worked for the Internal Revenue for years, I felt my job was secure. We packed hurriedly to catch the next train, hugged Sarinka's mama and told her we would return soon. After purchasing our tickets, we silently boarded the train. Suddenly I heard someone yelling, "Leon! Leon!" I peered out of the window to see my friend running alongside the stationary train with something in his hands. In our panic and haste to leave, we left a small suitcase at the ticket booth. I ran to the back of the train where there was an opening. My friend tossed it, and with outstretched arms I caught the small suitcase midair just as the train began to move. Smiling at the miraculous catch, I wondered if this was a lucky omen. Somehow, despite all the tumultuous events arising around us, we laughed in the moment and waved goodbye.

The next morning, dressed in my government uniform, I went to work not knowing what to expect. All was fine in Tuzla for two weeks. My supervisor summoned me to his office one day. Instantly my stomach churned. With a scowl on his face, this man who never reprimanded me before, shouted, "I know you're a Jew. Go home and wait for further instructions."

Surely my countenance showed a shock that couldn't be hidden, but I knew better than to respond with questions. Instead I obeyed and walked home slowly, my head hanging low with worry, wondering how I would explain this to Sarinka. Taking a deep breath, I opened the door.

"What happened? Why are you home already?" she asked, alarmed.

"I was told to go home and wait because they know I am a Jew. I wanted to ask what I was waiting for, but knew that wouldn't have been wise. Clearly, my position is in jeopardy."

"Oh my God! What are we going to do?"

I tried to soothe her, but had no words of comfort. I was just as frightened as she was. I realized that as her husband, I felt her pain more than my own. We sat for hours discussing what we should do.

The next morning a sudden knock at the door startled us. I opened it cautiously to find the postmaster with a letter addressed to me.

"Leon, what does it say?" Sarinka asked, noticing the expression on my face as I read.

"It's a letter informing me that I've lost my job. I must register as a Jew in this town and all Jewish men must report to a labor camp. I will NOT do that!" I yelled. "This is not even my hometown!"

"But what will happen if you don't?"

"We'll have to wait and see."

We had heard that the Germans invaded Sarajevo, the largest nearby city, on April 16th. They ransacked all eight of our local synagogues and obliterated priceless documents concerning Jewish life dating back to the 17th century and earlier. The Nazis destroyed most of the precious, sacred, and irreplaceable books and Torah scrolls, trying to erase our entire heritage.

Belgrade, the capital of Yugoslavia was bombed the next day, April 17, 1941, the Royal Yugoslav Army unconditionally surrendered to the Nazis and the members of the *Ustaša* joined them. Shortly after the country was divided. The Germans, led by Adolf Hitler would control the northeastern section of the country and the Italians, led by Mussolini, another dictator, would control the southwestern section.

Within two weeks of receiving my letter, the Nazis had completely occupied Tuzla. Life changed dramatically with new rules for all the Jewish people in Bosnia, the region of Yugoslavia where Tuzla, Travnik, and Žepče were all located. Our property no longer belonged to us. Sarinka and I lovingly furnished our new apartment together before the wedding with such excitement for our future. Suddenly nothing belonged to us anymore. Our radios were taken from us. We were commanded to wear a circular yellow badge with a Ž on it for Židov, Croatian for Jew. We were no longer free to walk around our own town at will. Jewish children's names were called off a list at school and teachers told them to leave and not come back. They could no longer play outside. Soldiers ordered us to walk in the middle of the roads while they paraded down our streets on horses. An imposed curfew forced us off the streets by six o'clock in the evening. We were horrified to witness firsthand what happened to those unwilling or unable to comply. They were arrested, severely beaten, or killed on the spot. Many of our non-Jewish friends no longer spoke to us or acknowledged us in passing. Everyday we waited for more terrible things to happen.

Rumors began to spread—too horrifying to believe they could possibly be true. We heard about Hitler and the laws he had imposed against Jews in Germany, but we never believed that it could happen to the people of Yugoslavia—we were a different story. We were a stubborn people and they weren't going to be able to take us quite so easily.

One day, we heard threatening pounding on our door. I reluctantly opened it. Two German soldiers in impeccable Nazi uniforms and shiny black boots stood staring at me, rifles by their side.

"Heil Hitler," they shouted while saluting. "Come with us, you dirty Jew! You have not reported to the camp as commanded."

"There must be some mistake," I told them. "I didn't register as a Jew here because this is not my hometown."

"Come with us NOW!" they ordered.

They grabbed my shirt and shoved me out of the house. I knew I didn't have a choice and certainly didn't want to be shot right there in front of Sarinka. For her sake I had to cooperate.

The shouted orders began as soon as I arrived at the labor camp. I washed the officers' laundry, and was forced to scrub public toilets, mopped the floors, and clean the streets. I knew I had to stay calm and typically I was a mild mannered man, but a volcano rumbled inside me, especially when they went back for Sarinka, forcing her to work there as well. She also cleaned the soldiers' bathrooms and scrubbed the floors of their offices. Having no choice, we did the work assigned to us for weeks, thankful that we could at least return home at the end of the day to comfort each other. Sarinka cried as she described how roughly the Nazis had treated her. Hearing this made me wonder if they would rape my beautiful bride after they watched her clean their offices? I spent every waking minute thinking about how to get out of this nightmare. I felt helpless and inadequate as her husband. This was no way to live.

I decided to contact some of the non-Jewish people I worked with to see if I could acquire special permits for us to return to Travnik. Luckily, they were not only co-workers, but also comrades who risked their well-being to obtain the papers for us that we needed. At least we would be out of harm's way temporarily at Sarinka's house, and she would be with her mama and Nonna. Although times were tense in Travnik, there was not a focused search for Jews at this point.

As soon as possible, Sarinka and I packed only what we could take in a small suitcase, leaving everything—all our new furniture and everything else we purchased to prepare for our marriage. We took the next train for what thankfully turned out to be an uneventful ride back to Travnik. However, upon arrival we were stunned to find that Sarinka's male friends from childhood had transformed into enemies, now supporting the *Ustaša*, who were as bad as (and some believed worse than) the Nazis. One day, a group of her former friends came to the house with a gun, threatening to kill her and her mother if they did not hand over their jewelry. Seeing the raw emotion on their faces made me sick as they surrendered their treasured possessions. Sarinka slowly handed over the precious pearls her mother had given her. Her mother relinquished her own wedding band as well as the one Sarinka's father wore and the watch he had given her.

I sat paralyzed, unable to protect my wife from this thievery as her former "friends" pointed their weapons at us. The jewelry wasn't enough. They proceeded to take Sarinka's beautiful mahogany grand piano that her father bought for her, which was more than she could bear. As she

Sarinka, standing by her piano, a gift from her father

sobbed, they took apart this precious gift and carried it out in pieces. I will never forget the feeling of paralysis and the disgust that filled me that day, but we knew we were lucky they hadn't killed all of us.

In addition to these acts of violence and thievery, the humiliation they caused, and my responsibility for Sarinka and her mother, I worried about my own mother. She had returned to Žepče on the day of our wedding for her safety. I had felt especially protective of her ever since my father died of cancer when I was only seven years old. Then, years later, my beautiful younger sister, Sarika, also died of cancer at the age of nineteen. My mother had endured such grief and loss, and I had taken care of her, even though I was the youngest boy of her surviving seven children: Five other boys, Elisha, Sevi, Josef, Avraham and Isaac, and two girls, Saphira and Solčika. All were married with two to four children of their own, and all owned stores until the Nazis took possession of them. I, on the other hand, never wanted to own a store like my siblings. All I wanted was to attend school and learn accounting. They could take away my job, but not my education. When I learned what had happened with their stores, I feared for how my family would survive.

"Sarinka, I need to go see my mother, brothers and sisters. I have to know if they are okay."

"Of course," she responded. "When?"

"As soon as possible," I answered.

"I'll pack a few things for us and we can leave today," she replied with sincere concern in her voice.

That evening we traveled by train, arriving safely in my hometown, Žepče. The heightened tension in the town was palpable. We overheard some of the whispered rumblings from other Jews around us and it was enough to make our insides tremble. I recognized an old friend of mine. "Nikko, tell me. What's going on? Are you hearing terrible stories, too?"

"Leon, if I told you what I heard it will sicken you."

"Tell me. I would rather know. It will help me make better decisions if I know what I'm facing. I'm not one to bury my head in the sand."

But never in my life could I have imagined the horrors I was about to hear.

"I heard that the *Ustaša* are training to become human butchers. Any man who cannot kill with joy would not be considered a true *Ustaša*. They got the young soldiers drunk, took them to the camp, and brought in young naked female Jewish prisoners. They instructed them to rape and kill the women to prove their callousness."

"Oh my God! I can't even imagine if they did that to Sarinka."

"Then I heard about another incident, a nineteen-year-old who protested he could kill men in battle, but not women and children. So one of the high-ranking commanders showed him how it was to be done. He ripped a two year old out of its mother's arms. He slit the throat of the child to demonstrate to the young soldier how to kill a baby, as others watched and laughed. The young soldier almost fainted when the child let out a gruesome scream and blood spilled everywhere. The young man was then ordered to kill the next toddler by smashing the child's head with his boot until he was dead. Afterwards, he got drunk and bragged about it. He assured everyone he would not need to drink to murder women and children in the future. He could do it now. Leon, people are saying so many were killed and thrown into the river that the water turned red."

"This is unbelievable! I heard the *Ustaša*'s mission was to help the Nazis rid the country of Jews, Gypsies, and Serbs, but this is ludicrous! We are not humans to them, but rodents they want to eliminate, and in such a barbaric manner. How did this happen? What can we do?"

Soon after hearing of all this horror, a notice came from the "Jewish Organization." (The Nazis forced this organization to make sure all the Jewish people obeyed their orders.) They advised the men and women of my town to pack a rucksack and be ready for deportation. We would be taken to a camp. Of course, we did not know anything about this "camp." Reluctantly I conformed, along with all the other Jews in my town. I had a terrible feeling about this—but the Jewish Organization instructed all of us to report. *Must be okay? No?*

A miracle happened. The train broke down along the way. Our departure was aborted, at least for that day. However, new directions from the Agency were issued—we were to report again on another designated day. What fate! I had fallen for this once, but I wouldn't do it a second time. I tried desperately to convince everyone to see it my way and begged them not to show up for the next train. My brothers, who had wives and children to worry about, felt they needed to listen and would follow the instructions given.

Instead, I decided to return to Sarinka's hometown, Travnik, and prepared to leave immediately. My mother came to the train station to see us off. I pleaded with her to come with us, but she refused. My heart still aches every time I think about that moment. I feared that my mother, this wonderful, good-hearted, righteous woman who gave of herself and took care of the sick in our town, would disappear from my life. We hugged and kissed. I gazed into her sweet face and beautiful sky-blue eyes always filled with kindness. I tried my best to commit them to memory. Tears flowed, as much as I tried to hold them back. I didn't want to let her go. I never wanted to forget the warmth of her embrace. I held her with all my love, feeling torn between my instinct telling me to flee with my wife and my desire to protect my mother. Down deep, I knew I may never see her again. Sarinka cried as she watched us and then she too hugged her goodbye.

I felt a rawness, deep down to the core of my very being, as I watched her fade away.

Such a sweet, amazing soul.

I can still see my mother, waving goodbye.

Simha Kabiljo (Leon's mother)

Chapter 6

Summer 1941

Before the rest of my family sadly did as they were instructed, I received a few postcards from my mother. They believed what they had been told: They packed a bag and went to a "camp" on a designated day. About fifteen Jewish families living in Žepče at that time took their last train ride when they dutifully reported to the station. Among those on the train were my grandmother, my mother, five of my brothers, my two sisters, and many nieces and nephews: About forty relatives in all.

In Travnik, with Sarinka's family, the Nazis trailed behind in their pursuit of us, but still we could feel the trepidation among neighbors when we saw one another. New restrictions were imposed on us. At least we could walk around until six o'clock in the evening. They forced us to walk in the middle of the street and they gave us rationed food. It became mandatory to wear a circular yellow badge with the Croatian letter Z, for Zidov meaning Jew. This way Jews were quickly and easily identified. I resented the officers and the Nazi soldiers who invaded our towns and our lives. The new "governor" of the town took over the newly furnished house of Sarinka's aunt who lived next-door to her and forced my

Circular yellow badge with the Croatian letter Z, for Zidov meaning Jew

mother-in-law to give his assistant a room in her home. Rumblings indicated that a camp had been built near Travnik. Conditions worsened by the day. We needed a plan. I wasn't going anywhere without one.

The Jewish Organization confirmed the news of a camp established in the area at *Kruščica*, a village near Travnik. Immediately they wanted to send bread to the workers in the camp, but it was difficult to find someone willing to take a chance on making this delivery. I volunteered with the president of the Jewish Organization so I could check out the situation with my own eyes, especially since I had heard rumors that they were killing people in the camp each day. With a horse and a wagon full of bread we proceeded apprehensively.

As I neared the camp I saw a group of about fifty men loading something onto wagons. I approached closer and closer. *Wait! Is that my brother, Isaac?* I had to do something, but I didn't want to let on that we knew each other. Someone could be watching, although I didn't see anyone as I looked around with forced nonchalance. *Could someone see from a watchtower?* I was a nervous wreck. While I tended to the bread delivery, he casually moved closer and closer to me. Taking a chance with both our lives, he managed to stealthily slip a small piece of paper into my hand as I continued unloading. We were so lucky no one saw. I didn't dare look at it.

Poor Isaac must have felt terribly helpless when they separated him from his wife and children, knowing they had also been forced to do hard labor. I wondered what would become of all of them.

As soon as we left the camp, I tentatively opened the note. The words were clear and simple: GET OUT BEFORE THEY CATCH YOU.

Travnik
Wednesday, October 15, 1941

ALL JEWISH MEN BETWEEN THE AGES OF 18 AND 60 MUST

REPORT TO JASENOVAC CAMP FOR WORK DETAILS.

"What now?" Sarinka asked me. "The officer living here will report you if you don't go on your own," she continued before I had a chance to answer.

"I don't think so," my mother-in-law quickly replied. "I have known him for a long time and he told me privately he will do whatever he can to protect us. He is a peaceful Muslim and he is against what the Nazis and the *Ustaša* are doing."

"Well, I can tell you one thing," I protested. "I will not give up so easily and go willingly just because they sent this. I will hide here until I figure out what else I can do."

Things had reached a point where I no longer left the house, and our family had become vigilant at all times for my safety. We had a plan in place just in case they came.

Sarinka's mother pulled me aside quietly. "Leon," she said, "I want you to have my husband's prayer books. He inscribed his name inside this little one. He would have wanted you to have them. He was a religious man like you. I am afraid you are going to need all the help you can get in the days ahead. They are small, so you can keep them with you always."

"Thank you. You don't know how much this means to me. I know Sarinka will also be very grateful to have something of her father's with us at all times. I promise to do my best to protect them, and her." These were the only words I could manage in response to this reverent gift that touched my heart so deeply.

My fingers lovingly caressed the brown leather cover of the books that my father-in-law had used to pray daily and I vowed to do the same.

A week passed. Considering the circumstances, all was as normal as possible. Sarinka and her mother still went out, though they were very careful not to violate the latest restrictions. One day, news spread of soldiers going door to door, conducting searches for men who didn't report. I knew I couldn't stay home, even though a thundershower was pelting the roof of the house. After much thought, I decided to go to the house of Sarinka's aunt, where the Bosnian governor of the town now forcibly resided. I thought this is the last place they would look for a Jew. In the pouring rain, I hid behind bushes and under a bench outside in the garden…for a long time. Success: I avoided capture.

The next morning, I stood near a window embraced in my prayer shawl. The Torah commands us to bind *Tefillin, while* davening our daily morning prayers. I had taken my time and with reverence for the biblical verses inscribed on the parchment scrolls inside, I wrapped one black leather box around the front of my head with the attached leather straps, and the other box on my left upper arm, facing my heart. The rest of the strap was wound around my arm seven times, extending down to my middle finger. With sincere intention, I prayed from my book, adding my own personal plea to help us survive.

My reprieve was short-lived. Sarinka's housekeeper, Katçia, a Muslim woman, glanced out the window and spotted a group of formidable Nazi soldiers approaching. "Oh my God! They're coming! Leon, go hide! Go hide!"

Hearing her cries, I had planned for this moment… always on edge and ready to jump and hide.

Please God help me out and save us.

I lifted my head when I heard Katçia's screams and heard them coming for me. I thought I had prepared myself, but when the time came, a barrage of fear hit me. Somehow, as if God had taken over, a burst of adrenaline and focus propelled me as I ran up to the attic. No time to remove my *Tefillin*. No time to think—just move! I positioned myself as far back as possible, under a large photograph, knowing full well my life depended on every I decision made. I heard a ruckus. I heard rifles beating on the front door.

My heart pounded so hard. *How could they not hear it?* Surely this would give me away.

Sarinka's mother answered the door and the shouting began immediately.

"Heil Hitler! Someone reported a Jew hiding in this house," one of the soldiers yelled as he burst through the doorway.

"Who told you such a thing?" my mother-in-law responded. I live here with my daughter

Start searching this house!" he commanded.

I couldn't believe this was happening. I started to shake as I crouched hugging the wall behind old relics stored there. My whole body quivered. I was soaked with sweat. I did the only thing I could do, believing this was the end, I prayed. Intuitively I began whispering the Shema. Then I struggled to keep each breath silent and not move a hair.

I heard more shouting. "How about the attic?"

Stomp…stomp…stomp…I heard them climbing the stairs, each thump gaining in intensity. Not only could I hear their footsteps, I could feel the floor shaking. Then, I felt their presence.

Can they smell my fear? Do they hear me breathing? God, please help me.

"Find him!" one screamed to another. "Take this stick. See if you can feel anyone."

I heard the sound of the stick, sharply striking everything including the wall—lots of commotion. Suddenly, I heard a crash as something tumbled down and covered my trembling body like a blanket thrown over a child playing hide and seek. *Was that it? Do they see me, even though I can't see them?* I couldn't risk moving. I would have to wait it out. The minutes seemed like hours.

Finally, they stomped down the stairs as roughly as they'd climbed them and left yelling that they would be back. I still sat petrified, unable to move. I needed to be absolutely sure no one stayed behind to trick me. I remained frozen in this position for what seemed like an eternity.

Once Sarinka was convinced they were gone, she ran upstairs and we held each other tightly, without saying a word. When I finally could speak, I explained what happened and we

both turned to look at what saved me. I couldn't believe my eyes. It was a huge photograph, over three feet by four feet, of Rabbi Avraham Abinun, a prominent rabbi in Travnik in the nineteenth century, who became chief rabbi of Sarajevo. We both knew who he was. Sarinka and I looked at each other with the same thought, as we stared at the image that had protected me and saved my life. Rabbi Avraham Abinun safeguarded me spiritually and physically. This was the rabbi that Sarinka's father admired so much that he hung his picture in his house. It was moved to the attic with the other religious items to protect the family in case the *Ustaša* came. No one could have predicted that moving this picture to the attic would have saved my life.

We were both happy, of course, but I knew this wasn't the end. I couldn't just sit there waiting for them to find me and realized at this point that I could no longer tempt fate. I needed a plan if Sarinka and I were going to survive. Many people were already fleeing, but I had no idea where or how they managed. Some were killed on the spot trying to escape.

I had to think of something.

Whatever it is, will be dangerous and risky.

God, please help me.

Chapter 7

Almost two months had passed since I went into hiding at Sarinka's house. We waited and waited, but we didn't know what we were waiting for. After many long hours of pondering how to proceed, I warily approached the governor's assistant who lived in our house. Risky as this was, I did not see any other option.

Earlier he'd told my mother-in-law he would try to help us. The majority of Catholics and Muslims in our town were on the side of the Germans, so we were very fortunate to have this particular Muslim man in our house. "Mr. Arnautović, I was wondering, could I have a few words with you, in private?" I asked, swallowing to moisten my dry mouth.

"What is it, Leon?"

"I'm sure I don't have to tell you things here are getting worse. It's only a matter of time until they find me and then they may come for Sarinka and her mother. I have a plan, but I need your help. I realize the magnitude of my request. I understand the risk involved for you, but I can't think of any other way out of this. Please just listen and see what you think." Not giving him a chance to respond, I continued. "I need five false passports and permission to travel for four others and myself. We would also need a covert way to get to the train station. If we could just get to Mostar we would be safe for a while, since it is an Italian-occupied zone and the Nazis are not there yet. We know Italy is an ally of Germany, but the treatment of Jews by them is not the same. Mostly, the Italians are of a different mindset—kinder and gentler. Once there, I could send for Sarinka and her mother."

I calculated this risk before I made the decision to approach him, resigned to the fact that all our hopes would rest on his answer. Silence followed. I sat staring at him, praying I hadn't misjudged the situation. *Would he instead turn me in?*

"You're asking an awful lot, you know. They could kill us all over this. Let me think about it and then I'll get back to you," he answered.

"Sure, I understand and I appreciate it. Let me know when you have your answer. Thank you for at least considering to help us."

Sarinka was waiting anxiously, aware I would be making this bold request. I went to her immediately and told her exactly what transpired. We were both apprehensive, wondering if he would turn us in for being so brazen as to ask this of him. But it was a chance we'd had to take. We could not go on like this, knowing the fate we thought awaited us if we did nothing.

At last, he summoned me to his room. My stomach churned as I approached. "Sit down," he began. "I looked into it. It will cost you though, especially for five of you. I got the five passports you requested with gentile names, and I arranged for a trustworthy well-connected Muslim to take you with a horse-drawn covered wagon to his house. You'll stay there and then someone else will come and take you to the station."

"Of course, no problem. Just tell me how much. I will tell the others and we will get you the money. We can't thank you enough. You're a good man."

"You are good people and I know it."

My traveling companions were to be Sarinka's uncles Davo and Yaakov, who had come from Italy to help with her father's store before he died, a student (the brother of one of Sarinka's friends), and a grocery store owner. I got in touch with them to make sure they were committed to this clandestine mission, to explain what we needed, and how it would take place. Our money would have to be sewn into our jackets. Preparations for the daring plan began.

How do I decide what are the essentials in my life that must come with me when I'm allowed so little and when I know how final it is? What are the chances of ever returning even if I do make it? I knew I would take the prayer books that belonged to Sarinka's father. I had to have those. I had to be careful because I was supposed to be going on a short business trip, so if my suitcase was opened it needed to reflect that. I had to be wise with my decisions.

I was on edge and needed rest, but I couldn't sleep knowing what faced me the next day.

December 15, 1941

Nothing was more painful than saying goodbye to Sarinka. We both knew we might never see each other again. We had plans in place for Sarinka to meet me, if I made it. But what if I didn't? Not knowing what the future held, we both tried to remain optimistic and avoided thinking of the alternative. We embraced as if we might never see each other again, because down deep we both knew that was a very real possibility. She cried. I pushed myself to stay strong. I knew I needed to do this for her because if I let my emotions go as well, I wouldn't have been able to leave at all. I gave her one more hug and kiss and then I walked out the door as bravely as possible. Inside I was crying like a baby.

It was a blustery, cold winter night. The Muslim man arrived around midnight with his horse and wagon. With the substantial currency transaction completed a few days prior, we had no choice but to trust him. I looked up at the bleak colorless sky and whispered a prayer under my breath before climbing into the wagon, where I tried to lie as flat as possible. The man covered the five of us with the straw he used to shield his merchandise from the weather. The horses trotted along. We quivered at the sounds of the night, not knowing when and if we would be exposed.

To our amazement, no one stopped us. We arrived safely at his house. Shivering as much from fear as the cold, we silently climbed out of the wagon, each whispering thanks to the stranger. *So far, so good.*

The five of us entered the house cautiously. The man barely spoke. He just pointed to the floor space where we could sleep until the early morning hours, when the second man would pick us up by car and take us to the train station in Sarajevo.

The next morning in the car no one spoke. My mind wandered to thoughts of leaving my mother and now Sarinka, wondering where it would all end. The silence, as we drove on, spoke only of our terror. What would we do if anything went wrong?

Using our false papers, we purchased tickets for Mostar with a sigh of relief. I was ready to board the train as Ivan Jelinović.

We knew we would be killed if we were caught. To an outside observer, we appeared as ordinary travelers, casually sitting and waiting for the train.

"We should sit separately on the train," I suggested to my friends, "Each in a different car. That way we all have a chance to survive, independently of one other." It made sense and everyone knew it, but we were scared to do this alone. After some discussion, we all agreed.

The train finally arrived. We boarded separately, each in a different coach as planned. On boarding, I went through each car, taking a seat in the last one. I tried to look as normal as possible, hoping my thoughts wouldn't give me away. We traveled for a couple of hours until the train stopped at the border dividing the Nazi-occupied area of Yugoslavia with the Italian-occupied zone. The stop dragged on much longer than I expected. I wondered what was going on. My only thought was to silently remind myself to stay calm, look calm, and act calm. There was no reason to think that we would not make it if we had come this far, but this long stop made me very nervous. We were so close. We had to get through this border check.

I looked out the window, stunned and horrified. Two Nazis with their vicious, barking dogs had taken all four of my travel companions off the train. They screamed orders and then roughly pushed them with their rifles, laughing at the horrified faces of my companions. I tried not to think of the death they faced. I sat staring out the window thinking that surely I would be next. *Had they been questioned about traveling with anyone else? Had authorities asked about me?*

Not showing any emotion now would be my greatest test of all.

I jerked at the sudden sound of the train car door as it forcibly opened. Two Nazis marched imperiously—directly to me. Their perfect uniform and shiny black boots could not disguise the monsters I saw as they approached. My heartbeat accelerated, pounding as loud as the defiance I felt toward them. "Your papers," one demanded. I tried my hardest to appear unemotional and with a surprisingly steady hand I turned over the passport with the name Ivan Jelinović. "Where is your photo?" he shouted in a raucous tone.

Luckily I didn't look Jewish and spoke with no trace of Jewish accent in my native tongue. I appeared calm and fluently replied, "I was in such a hurry for this very important business trip, I was informed that I could leave without it." My heart pounded. He stared at me and I stared right back at him. Inside I trembled, but I heard myself speak fluent Serbian, strong and powerful with no apprehension. It was as if God gave me extraordinary powers to look him straight in the eyes, and as if someone else spoke for me—almost startling myself. *Where was this strength coming from?*

Their stares cut into me a second time, but I stared back—this time with an insolent glare, as if insulted. They finally moved on.

In a stupor I sat, barely able to breathe or believe all that just happened. My mouth was parched while thoughts raced through my mind, but I managed to sit still and impassive for the remainder of the trip. I was in shock.

At last, I arrived safely in Mostar, but felt no relief. I felt sick. What gave my travel companions away? Could it have been that they "sounded" Jewish or their fear openly showed? I have no idea what gave them away, but I felt terribly guilty and spent many hours pondering their fate and why I alone survived. I dreaded the thought of writing to Sarinka. I hated for her to bear the burden of informing the other families of such devastating news. Even though I knew she would of course be comforted knowing I survived, telling her that only I made it safely while the others surely faced death, brought with it a heaviness and guilt like I've never experienced.

Part Three

Sarinka

Chapter 8

Leon left on December 15, 1941. Saying goodbye to him made me realize how much I loved him. How could our love have grown so strong in such a short time? He left me with sweet tender kisses. Sobbing after our last embrace, I tried desperately to hold on to love I felt from him. I could see right through Leon's stoic façade as he slowly stepped out the door. My insides reeled and clenched as I gasped each breath, my heart pounding to get out and leave with him. My eyes followed him until he was out of sight.

Days passed. No news.

I ached just thinking about him. Already emotionally exhausted, the waiting made my nerves raw. Mama did her best trying to calm me, but she knew all too well the possibilities we faced.

Finally… "I received a letter from Leon! This means he made it!" I exclaimed. My hands shook making it difficult to open the envelope. My mother came running, as anxious as I was to hear the news.

"Oh my God! Oh my God!" was all that came out of my mouth as I read it. Tears flowed instantly.

"What is it, Sarinka?" Mama asked fearfully as she sat down to brace herself.

"Leon is the only one who made it. The Nazis took the others away. I must get word to their families." His letter told the whole story. The more I read, the more anxious I became. After taking in his final words, I handed the letter to my mother.

Relieved and grief-stricken all at once, I knew how close I had come to losing my husband. At the end of the letter he told me I must come to Mostar immediately. Leon wrote, "Just find a way to do this and get word to me about the arrangements immediately."

My mother and I took the letter to Aunt Sarina and her sons so they could read first hand about Uncle Yaakov's fate. They cried and we cried with them. Never could I have imagined I would have to deliver such devastating news to my aunt and cousins—making this one of the most emotionally difficult moments of my life. Uncle Davo never married but Aunt Sarina would tell those close to him.

My mother assured me she would tell the families of the merchant and student as soon as possible. She also spoke to the assistant governor again, and once more he agreed to help. This time the false papers were for me. Immediately, I wrote Leon telling him the plan. I would go as Zulka, the daughter of my father's very close friend, Ibro Ibrahimović, a Turkish Muslim.

Zulka offered me her own clothes to wear: an ornate headscarf, a bright Turkish blouse and a dress in shades of red, purple, green and gold. Most important, though, was the veil she gave me to obscure my face because I "looked" Jewish.

Ibro demonstrated such loyalty to my family. He not only worked for my father, but they also shared a close friendship. He continued to help my family in the store after my father died. This remarkable man chose to help me, the only daughter of his good friend, now deceased for ten years. Ibro Ibrahimović would not sit back and watch what was happening. This righteous Muslim man decided to help save my life at great peril to himself and his loved ones.

So now, with a plan, came the reality of leaving. *What about my mother? How could I possibly leave her?*

"Mama, of course I appreciate all that you did to arrange this for me, but I'm scared. I'm scared to go, scared to leave you and Nonna, scared of what life will be like after I walk out the door. Please, please come with me. I'm begging you."

"Sarinka, don't worry. Go with your husband now. That is your place. Mine is to stay with my mother. She is too old to make the trip and we would only endanger your safety. It will all be over soon. You'll probably be back in three or four weeks. Let's hope…."

"Mama," I pleaded through my tears, "I can't leave you. I just can't. Please, please come with me."

"What are they going to do to two old ladies? We'll be here when you return, when everything gets back to normal. But now, Sarinka, you must go."

I wanted so badly to believe her, but I knew her every word was meant to push me onward, to choose my husband over my mother—*How could I choose between the two people I loved most in the world?*

January 7, 1942

Sarinka, dressed as daughter of a Turkish Muslim

Uneasily, I dressed in Zulka's clothes. I put on an extra sweater under the brightly colored blouse and dress she gave me, not only for a better fit, but also to serve as an extra layer for the bitter cold I would face. Mama walked towards me with a heavy sigh, holding Zulka's scarf. With not one word uttered, she folded the cream scarf with the colorful trim twisted around, making it more decorative. She placed the folded edge above my forehead, with only a bit of my hair exposed and tied the ends in back at my neck to cover another Jewish trait, my curly hair. Now conscious of my own heavy breaths, I donned a heavy winter coat.

My heart ached as I walked toward Nonna, her wrinkled face and heavy eyes filled with more pain than I could bear to see. Neither of us said a word. I hugged her, not wanting to let go, and kissed her goodbye as my tears overflowed again.

Then my mother came to me with Zulka's veil in her hands. I started to tremble and the tears stung my face. With an even fiercer grasp than I held Nonna, I wrapped my arms around this woman who had always loved, supported, and sacrificed so much for me, knowing it was this intense love that gave her the fortitude to push me to leave.

Within seconds, so many thoughts raced through my head. Gone was all the resentment I harbored when she left me alone with the servants after Tata died and went out with new suitors. She was so young when she'd lost her husband and must have been so lonely. I reflected on all the precious time I wasted and the aggravation I caused her with school, piano, and my lack of ambition after high school—time I may possibly never have with her again. How could I have been so self-absorbed?

I know I have to do this, but how can I? What if I never see her again? I am not ready to move on without her in my life. There are so many questions I still needed to ask her. I feel so close to her now.

I moved in slow motion, trying to etch each moment in my memory. Ibro, who was undoubtedly nervous himself, urged us on, reminding us of the time. My mother gently and carefully attached the veil that covered my face. Now she hugged me while quietly weeping. Her strength collapsed.

I felt queasy dressed in this disguise, like an impostor. I trembled and sobbed, making no effort to hide my emotions. Somehow I would have to find the courage to go through with this perilous plan.

My mother embraced me once more, enveloping my entire being with her love. I hoped it would give me the resilience I needed to survive. I was unwilling to let go. I stood there choking on each breath as I stared into her tear filled eyes, as blue as the Adriatic Sea. I will never forget that moment. I held her soft hands in mine, trying desperately to commit the feeling of her skin to memory. I needed to preserve the sound of her voice, her sweet scent, and her warmth and love that I had always taken for granted. I needed to etch it all into my mind so I would never forget.

My mother's soft comforting voice interrupted my thoughts. "Sarinka, you must go. I know it's hard, but you need to go to Leon now and we will see each other later—maybe three or four weeks. Ibro is waiting and you'll miss the train if you don't go now."

Refusing to believe that I would never see her again, I turned and assured her, "I will see you soon." For some reason saying it out loud made it feel as though it would come true. I could not leave thinking otherwise. I hugged her with all my heart one last time as I wept. Haltingly I followed Ibro Ibrahimović out the door.

Turning around every few seconds, I captured my last glimpses of where I was from—my loved ones, my house, my town. I thought of our three housekeepers, the assistant governor, and all who helped us and protected us from those who preferred us dead. I watched as my mother and Nonna waved goodbye, their images grew dimmer and dimmer. Sadness pulled at my heart like a magnet. I wanted to turn around and run back, but I continued walking with Ibro, each step heavier and harder to take. Tears flowed as I continued to question my choice to leave my mother, Nonna, my friends, my hometown, and my identity—to run and hide with my husband amid our uncertain future.

I never saw any of them again.

Chapter 9

Original painting of Mostar by Sarinka.

January 7, 1942

We arrived at the Sarajevo train station bound for Mostar, filled with anxiety over the risky plan to reunite with my husband and the consequences if it didn't work.

I boarded the train, took a seat next to Ibro, and tried to look as inconspicuous as possible. We had a few very cold hours ahead of us. Even with the frigid temperature, I broke out into a sweat. Vomit was just a breath away. Ibro insisted I wear my heavy winter coat. Perspiration dripped as I looked out, wondering how this surreal scene would run its course. The wheels of the train screeched as they began to turn.

An ivory blanket covered the mountains and icicles dripped from the trees. Waves of snow blurred the chalk-streaked sky. I stared at the crystal shards hanging from the branches as we rode along the rugged terrain with tunnels and viaducts. The view looked like an artist's rendering. On any other day, I would have marveled at this scene, but nothing felt picturesque about this setting. *How could such evil be embedded in such a beautiful place?* Silently, I mourned.

The train came to a halt at the next station. New sounds could be heard. Soldiers boarded and I immediately thought of Leon's experience. Ibro felt my clammy hands tremble against his own. He wrapped his arm around me with a squeeze. Quietly he whispered, "Sarinka, avoid looking up at their faces, but if they should approach us, look up and give them that warm smile you always gave me when you came into the store. It will be vague through your veil, but you'll appear calm."

"I don't know if I can do that."

"You have no choice. If you want to see Leon again you will find the strength."

The soldiers' heavy footsteps grew nearer. I couldn't breathe.

No, not now. Get it together. Be strong. Leon did it. I can too.

They stopped before us and asked Ibro to show his papers. I lifted my head and mustered up a shy smile.

The soldiers seemed indifferent, hurried. "Who is this young woman traveling with you?" one of them asked Ibro.

"This is my daughter. We are going to Mostar to meet my sister and her daughter."

I looked up and smiled wide, again hoping it would somehow convey a relaxed appearance. He looked me over for what seemed the longest minute of my life, then continued to the next person. I looked up at Ibro, but of course I couldn't say a word. We rode on in silence.

As soon as we arrived at Mostar, I went to the lavatory and removed my scarf and veil. I thought of one thing only, finding my husband whom I hadn't seen in weeks. Scanning the station for Leon, I suddenly spotted him. As if he felt my gaze, he turned toward me. With great control, we cautiously walked toward each other so as to not draw undue attention. He held me as I quietly wept, unable to speak. We strode in silence, holding hands firmly. There would be plenty of time to talk later, but for now anxiety gripped every part of me.

Ibro purchased his ticket for the train ride back to Travnik and then came to say goodbye. I hugged this brave, kind, selfless man whom I had never hugged in my life. "Ibro, how can I ever thank you? I'll pray for your safe return and hope to see you again when this is all over. I can never repay you for risking your life for me. I will be forever grateful."

Ibro embraced me as if I truly was his daughter. "I'll tell your mother and Nonna that I left you in Leon's arms. This will ease their minds. Be strong, Sarinka. Perhaps we will see each other again some day." With that, he turned and walked toward the train.

Mostar was one of the most strikingly beautiful cities in Yugoslavia, and at its heart was the beautiful sixteenth century Ottoman bridge made from a pale stone that reflected the glow of the sunset. Stari Most (Old Bridge), as it is known, extended over the River Neretva and connected the two parts of the city. My parents and I had always admired it. We went there to celebrate my birthday one year and watched as daredevils jumped with excitement from the Old Bridge into the river. What special memories—a happy little girl enjoying a July holiday with both her parents—and how sad to be here under such different circumstances.

We continued to walk arm in arm without a word until we arrived at the guesthouse where Leon had already rented a room. I longed to share my memories of this city with him, but didn't have the emotional strength to discuss anything.

My eyes scanned the sparsely furnished guest room, noticing the frozen water in the pitcher and the frost on the windows. This was just the beginning of my adjustment to a new lifestyle.

Mostar—now occupied by the Italians—may have been a bit safer for us, but it was not going to be easy. The first night was especially difficult. Leon sensed my mood. "Sarinka, talk to me. Tell me how you got here. Saying goodbye to your mother and Nonna must have been heartbreaking."

As soon as my words came so did the tears. "Leon, I only dreamt of reuniting with you, but a sick feeling from leaving home is still with me. Deep down I don't think I'll ever see my mother and Nonna again. Ibro escorted me here, but fear was my true companion, sitting closer to me than I would have liked—fear of never seeing my mother again, fear of not reaching you, fear of what will happen next, and fear to say all this out loud."

"Of course, Sarinka. I understand. That is why we must depend on each other and be patient. Our journey will be tough, tougher than either of us can probably imagine, but we must focus on the future and making it through this together, no matter what. Promise me you will try to be strong."

"I promise, but you will have to help me. I'm not sure I can do this."

Leon held me the whole night. We shivered in the cold room and hardly slept, with too much sadness for one day, too many worries, and no way to escape these thoughts.

In the morning, we awoke feeling more tired than before going to bed, but the security of being in Leon's arms helped comfort me. We left the room to try to get some coffee and a bite to eat, discussing how we should walk, and trying our best not to be noticed. Holding hands, we sauntered as if on a casual stroll, but we made sure not to make eye contact with anyone or start any conversations. Leon had already made some connections with Jewish organizations that were trying to help refugees. They told us there were many in need, but we could come there daily for what little food they could spare. Very weak coffee and stale bread started our day. The frigid temperature was brutal and both of us had already lost weight from all the stress, making us feel even colder. We walked back to our room, talked and slept, slept and talked. What was there for us to do? We were afraid to go on too many walks, so we ventured out only to get food.

We had nothing. I had moments when my mind wandered to a time when I not only owned, but played, my own beautiful mahogany baby grand piano. Now, it merely seemed like a dream. So, with little money and sparse food handouts, we went on and on like this for about nine harsh months.

Rumors buzzed of the Nazis coming closer, so we knew staying in Mostar was no longer an option. Always trying to be a few steps ahead of the Germans, Leon stealthily searched for a new plan. The waiting in Mostar would have to end, though we had no idea what lay ahead for us.

Leon took his intuition seriously. The time had come to make a move. His mind never deviated from knowing that we would survive all of this. This strength and conviction, along with his unwavering belief in God guided every decision. He refused to entertain the horrible outcomes that constantly played out in my mind. Often Leon would tell me, "Sarinka, think good and it will be good. Please, please do this for me." All I could tell him was that I would try.

We managed to get a truck ride to Montenegro, a province, which at this time was an occupied territory under the military government of Fascist Italy, also known as the "Italian puppet state." Deep into Montenegro, Serbian Chetniks, a detachment of the Yugoslav Army, targeted the Yugoslav communist partisans. Surprisingly, they took in Jews. We were told, "If you are not communists, you can stay."

Leon responded sincerely, "Believe us, please. We are not communists. We are just trying to save ourselves from the Nazis."

We succeeded in finding lodging in an overcrowded area, complete with a food shortage, of course. With the arrival of summer we took long walks, but did so cautiously. With political tension in the air and armed conflicts all around us, we never felt safe. We congregated with other Jews whenever we could. Everyone wanted the same answers: news of what may be happening in their town, news of their families, and news of Hitler's camps. We heard stories about Jews who were supposedly having good times in the camps, and that the Nazis allegedly had film to prove it. We didn't know what to believe anymore. After two or three weeks, we did not feel safe there either. The Nazis were approaching and would reach Montenegro soon, or so we heard. Worst of all was the constant fear that accompanied us every moment of every day.

Leon was consumed with each choice he made to help us survive. One day, with a heavy sigh, he said, "I know we haven't been here long, but we need to move again. It's not safe to stay. I am so scared for both of us.

I feel responsible that I sent for you, but Sarinka, you have to believe that I thought it was the best thing to do. It would have been worse for you if you stayed with your mother."

"Leon, I am here now. We're in this together and I don't care how many times we move. I trust your decisions and we must hope and pray now that somehow we will be guided through this. Listen to your instincts and we will do whatever you think is best."

'We could go to Split, which is also controlled by the Italian Army, but in order to do this, we need legal papers. What do you think?"

"I told you. I'll do whatever you decide."

Leon met with the Serbian Cheniks the next day and told them our plan to leave and travel to Split but we needed legal passports to do so. They agreed—probably happy to have two less refugees in their way. We took a train and then traveled by boat north along the coast to Split. We spoke very little, trying not to bring any attention to ourselves. With no questions asked of us, we considered ourselves very fortunate that we made it and would be safe for the time being.

September 1942

A month later, tension between the Italians and Germans mounted. Warnings were sent to the Italians demanding their support to deport the Jews. Mussolini signed a document, "nulla osta," –*There is no opposition*. This meant a huge collection of Jewish refugees would be put directly in the hands of the Germans, or maybe even worse to the "wild men of the *Ustaša*" knowing they would be killed, but several Italian Army commanders, two of whom were General Marion Roatta, Commander of the 2nd Army and Giuseppe Pièche, General of Carabinieri Forces, thankfully rejected this order and refused to comply. *Thank God for these Italians.*

It was so frightening. The Nazis targeted Split with bombs as they came closer and closer. We found ourselves more on edge than ever, wondering where we would be safest. When we walked outside sometimes we had to run for cover. We watched the destruction of Split little by little and prayed that we would not be among the victims.

Fortunately, I had a relative in Split, Julius Broner, who had become very wealthy from a successful shoe business. He took us both in, since he was very close to my father and would do what he could to protect us. I finally felt some comfort knowing we were with family.

Julius's grown daughter, Pepića, an intelligent girl who had been educated in London, invited a small group to her house one evening. She was young and beautiful, so full of life. Not a typical Yugoslavian brunette, she was blonde, blue eyed and fair skinned. It felt so foreign to see her standing before us, ready to lead. Where? We did not know.

The meeting was quiet and clandestine. We were lucky to have her father as our sentinel who would alert us if anyone came uninvited. One by one we quietly entered the house. Leon couldn't wait to hear what she had to say. We sat whispering softly to one another, swapping speculations as we waited for her to begin.

"I was put in contact with a man named Meyer, who is in charge of a resistance group. He suggested that I have this meeting and encourage any of you interested to come to the mountains and join him. He said it is rough, and only for the young and strong, but at least we wouldn't be waiting here for God knows what."

As a brave leader, Pepića continued, "It isn't good. We must get out of here. The German army is closely approaching. Hitler and his followers are condemning innocent Jewish people and others to 'resettlement' or 'work camps' where it is rumored he is eventually murdering all who enter. Meyer, a friend of mine from Sarajevo, told me all that he is hearing. He joined the resistance group fighting in the mountains, with the Yugoslav partisans, also known as the People's Army. Josip Broz Tito is the top commander. Their goal is to see an independent Socialist Yugoslavia, using guerrilla warfare. Most of these armed civilians are young, like us. They decided to fight like free people even though the odds are against them. In their own small way, they are making it harder for the Germans. They have blown up convoys, sabotaged trains carrying supplies, and they've even destroyed Nazi power plants and factories. We can't just sit here like sheep waiting for slaughter. I won't do that. My sister Deborah is in, too. Who's with us?"

Leon didn't hesitate and quickly responded, "Sarinka and I are in! What do the rest of you think?" Everyone listening, spirited and naïve as we all were, decided to join the partisans. Pepića contacted Meyer, the commander of the group, and arrangements were made.

As the time to leave Julius's grew nearer, Leon and I went over and over our decision, knowing it was the best choice, but it didn't suppress the terror we felt deep inside. In fact, it made it worse.

We met Meyer at the base of the mountain after dark and covertly proceeded up the path, following him, walking with nothing but the clothes we wore and what little we had stuffed in our pockets. Thankfully, Leon still had my father's prayer books. I wondered how I would get through this in a dress and shoes not meant for hiking, but they were all I had. The few elderly who wanted to join us were loaded on the one truck we had temporary use of and the rest of us walked scared and apprehensive with only our hope tucked away. We were acutely aware of the birds all around us. The leaves rustled beneath our feet as we approached a bridge on the way up to the mountains. We all knew the possibility of unidentified mines that could have been left there from other resistance groups before us. Step by step we gingerly walked, not knowing what we might happen upon. Suddenly we heard explosions. With horror, we looked up as Nazi planes came into view, dropping bombs, targeting the nearby bridge. Meyer shouted for everyone to get down.

I looked at the mud in the ditch. Laying down in my dress was not an option for me. I stood petrified. I heard desperate voices yelling, "Get down you crazy woman! Get down NOW!" Still like a stubborn, spoiled child, I refused to lie down in the sludge and ruin the only dress I owned. I knew it was stupid, but I could not get myself to move. If Leon had been closer, he probably would have yanked me down and thrown himself on top of me for protection.

The bridge blew up and people were injured. I stood unscathed, realizing how lucky I was to be alive.

The wounded were loaded onto the truck and hurriedly we pushed it through the shallow water. We followed, trudging across and hoping to go unnoticed. We needed to get help fast. The rest of us traipsed by foot deep into the mountains. We walked and walked for hours.

Meyer finally found his group of partisans. An international Red Cross group worked side by side with them, and they quickly aided the injured. So much was happening all around me. *Mama would be horrified if she knew where I was and how close I had come to death.*

The Yugoslav Partisans—Serbs and Jews—shared a hatred for the Nazis, since they targeted both groups with such cruelty. We all wanted freedom and an end to the slaughter, but Jews had an extra enemy; some of the partisans hated us, too. Meyer instructed, "Don't ask too many questions, or you may be accused of spying."

These crude resistance fighters were students, teachers, lawyers, doctors, shop owners, and even children trying to survive. They blew up Nazi trains, and stole rifles and food. They knew if captured, severe torture would precede their deaths. Their captors would try to make them divulge secret information about partisan attacks and plans, which would surely lead to more deaths. They were prepared to commit suicide or die fighting for their lives rather than surrender to Hitler's inhumane plans.

We were proud to be a part of this courageous group during such a dangerous time, even if there were bad feelings toward us among some of the partisans. With Meyer as our leader, the rest of us took on other necessary jobs. My job was to work with the Red Cross. Someone came over and shouted at me, "Put these brogans on. You'll be working hard. Now you're a nurse." I threw my heels into the woods after the Red Cross worker handed me the durable coarse brown leather ankle-high shoes.

We set up a makeshift hospital in the woods wherever we were. We built operating tables out of large thick tree branches and used a kitchen knife for digging bullets out of wounds. I did the best I could with what little knowledge I had. They told me my job was to keep the wounded alive, to bring them back to life because they were needed to fight. The one thing I was good at was following orders. They gave me alcohol or vodka to cleanse the wounds. I learned a lot medically, talked to patients, gave them hope, and tended to their needs. At the end of the day I washed blood-soaked bandages because we all knew tomorrow they would be needed again. I boiled the shirts of those who died to use for additional bandages. If the Partisans didn't die from battle injuries or gangrene, they died of typhoid, or infection from being infested with lice. It was all so hard to witness, but I felt useful and each day took on new meaning.

Leon was expected to carry a gun and become a soldier. He tried, but he was very uncomfortable with it. One evening he confided in me: "I know this sounds terrible, but I don't want the responsibility of a gun. I can't do this. You know I can't shoot an animal, much less a person. It's not my nature, and with no training I will be a sitting duck. How can I be a fighter? I've never fought in my life."

Leon knew nothing of my next move. I avoided confrontations whenever possible but could not let this happen. "Leon, I'll be back soon," I told him, leaving abruptly. Using every ounce of courage I had, I stormed up to Meyer, yelling and crying. "Leon can't be one of your soldiers. He doesn't have it in his heart to kill. He knows nothing about shooting or guns. Please, Meyer. Please."

"Sarinka, calm down. No one here does. We all have to do what we can to survive. We need him."

"Meyer, I left everything and everybody behind. I can't lose my husband now. Please, please find another way for him to help. Leon doesn't know I'm here and he will probably be furious with me, but I just can't lose him now. We just got married. Please, Meyer. He'll work hard some other way. He'll do anything you say."

"All right, but he'll have to do other work whether he likes it or not. He can help clean up, keep fires going, and bring people water. He'll have to do whatever needs to be done."

"Thank you. Thank you. He'll gladly do that. I know he will help in any way he can."

When Leon heard what I'd done, he couldn't believe I had the audacity to confront our leader, but he was sincerely thankful and gladly accepted whatever task was demanded of him to help at the campsite. He helped the Red Cross with the wounded soldiers, carried water, cleaned guns, and did whatever physical labor they asked of him.

For the next four months we camped in the mountains. We were told the forest was our protection: No forest, no partisans. The forest safeguarded us and without it we wouldn't have been able to push against the Nazis as we did. We stole grapes from vines as we trekked into the emptiness of the night, many of us carrying heavy medical equipment since we had no cars or trucks to help us. Each day it was someone's job to forage for food and then it was all divided evenly. The farmers among the group knew how to cover our tracks so the Nazis wouldn't be able to track and hunt us down. We proclaimed that we were different from the Nazis because although we may have stolen a cow to be shared by all, they stole all the livestock. We ate grapes, figs and berries off the trees and slept on green woolen blankets covering a mattress of packed leaves. We slept right out in the woods whether it snowed or rained or temperatures dropped. The sky was our roof and the ground our bed. We could easily have been swallowed by the hollowness and sadness we felt, but we created our own light with hushed nocturnal conversations. We would not be sucked into the darkness by the fear that constantly pulsed through us.

Rumblings of the Nazis coming closer again tormented me. My nights were haunted with dreams of them sharpening their claws and silently swooping me up like an owl attacks its prey. We did not have much ammunition and I witnessed many die from typhus due to the unsanitary conditions. I hated the scant showers, the lack of privacy and clean clothes. My menstrual period stopped from my poor diet. Pallid skin replaced my lightly blushed cheeks. The lack of nutrition took its toll on all of us as we languished in the unforgiving cold of the mountains, trying our best to survive in the frigid forest now that winter was here.

One day, among the numerous partisans in the forest, Leon came across an old friend from Sarajevo. " Leon, you're not a soldier and I bet Sarinka can barely tolerate this. Save your lives—have children so we can have more people who are Jewish in the world when this is all over. I will help you get to Korcula, an island off the Adriatic coast. You and the others who don't have the animal instinct needed to fight will go there. Other partisans are there who will help you live."

"Thank you so much, but how can we leave all of you? You have been so good to us. We probably wouldn't be alive now if not for this group of partisans."

"Leon, we have to hope someone will survive to tell our story. We have already decided you should go to Korcula with some of the others and we hope and pray you will be safe there."

Leon found Meyer to tell him of our decision. "Meyer, how can we ever thank you? We hope we will see you again some day. We both thank you sincerely and hope we will make it to tell this story one day—not only to our children, but to all who will listen."

"I understand, Leon. May God be with you," Meyer responded.

I knew by now to trust Leon's instincts. When he told me what his friend from Sarajevo said, we both agreed to follow his advice. So we gathered our few belongings, said our goodbyes, cried and hugged one another. We left with the words, "Hope we meet again," and "Good luck."

The cat and mouse chase continued as we moved again at the end of that year. The Nazis were now approaching as they prepared to occupy Vela Luka, located on the western side of Korcula. We grew more aware of people disappearing. It always led to thoughts of my own mother, and I continued to worry about her and other family members every day. With no confirmation of their deaths, I still had hope.

One cold winter day, we heard a lot of excitement. Small boats piloted by British sailors arrived. Everyone cheered when they saw them. I just stood there, not knowing what this meant, but then I realized they had come to help us. For the first time, I felt God heard my prayers and someone was coming to save all of us from the Nazi terror. We heard rumors of Hitler's evil machinations. The British fighters offered hope of survival. They gave us candy and ensured our safety. They were instructed to take us to Vis, the farthest inhabited Croatian island, in the Adriatic Sea. It was a small island off the mainland of Yugoslavia with many sick people, but we knew we had to escape the Nazi terror that began escalating in Korcula.

One by one, the soldiers carefully helped us onto their small boats. We purposefully left in the middle of the night to avoid German patrols. I was scared but knew we would be safer anywhere than here. Leon and I sat huddled together, trying to keep each other warm from the gusty winds. Just feeling his body against mine calmed me. We were leaving together and that was all that mattered at the moment.

Chapter 10

As 1942 drew to a close, we arrived safely on the island of Vis, with an approximate area of only 35 square miles and the only one not under Nazi rule. Vis was covered in lush vegetation with everything from pine trees to palm trees, carob trees and vineyards. We trudged up and down rocky and hilly parts, exploring. The natives of the island had their family land marked off by three foot high stonewalls, wide enough for someone to walk on top—and at times we did, just to add some diversion to our day.

Italian forces, British soldiers, Yugoslav partisans and eventually American soldiers occupied the island of Vis, all with the same goal—to stop the Germans. After we arrived, Josep Broz Tito, the Yugoslav Partisan leader, commanded the soldiers not to mingle with the Yugoslav Partisan women. Given military dresses to wear, we were explicitly instructed not to even talk to American or British soldiers or we would be sent for combat duty ourselves. Leon didn't have to worry about me following that order. I was too scared to speak to anyone but him. The Yugoslav women were not flirtatious and kept their distance from the soldiers as asked.

Minimal tent-like barracks were set up for us, each holding fifteen people. We slept on straw-lined bunk beds covered with burlap remnants from empty food bags. We existed. We helped with farming when needed. Everyone pitched in to keep the place as clean as we could despite the crowded conditions. During the warm months we occasionally ate fresh fruit grown on the island, but usually we had bean soup, bread, and potatoes.

Although Leon and I had only each other, we knew a few acquaintances from our hometowns. For fifteen long months with strict curfews, we occupied ourselves with our menial jobs, lots of idle waiting, walking, talking, and wondering what the future would hold. Those who knew English tried teaching others, but our most urgent challenge: avoid the German bombs. We had no idea Vis was one of the most important outposts of the war. Refugees were among the casualties but babies were also born.

February 1944

The British sent more soldiers and doctors who quickly set up hospitals to treat the wounded among the British, the partisans, and even the civilians. As time went on, more and more refugees joined us and more troops arrived. Water and food supplies became scarce. We were given only bread and SPAM, which we learned was spiced ham that Jews were religiously forbidden to eat. We ate minimal amounts to survive. Witnessing people die of disease broke my heart and sadly became more rampant due to the overcrowded conditions.

One day Leon voiced his concerns. " I'm really worried about you, Sarinka. Don't think I haven't noticed you speak less, eat less, and seem apathetic to everything and everyone around you."

"I'm sorry, Leon. There is no controlling what's going on inside of me. My only goal is to survive from one day to the next. This is the only way I know how to deal with it all. If my emotions surface, I will break. Please just let me be."

With this said, Leon understood how fragile I was and that it was best to let me get through it the only way I knew how: unresponsive to all.

March 5, 1944

The situation on the island grew desperate, with 15,000 refugees and civilians in constant danger. Brigadier Tom Churchill, Winston Churchill's second son, arrived and took charge of the island. To protect the civilians, the British decided to relocate partisans ages fifteen to fifty to a temporary transit station in Santa Croce, Italy. Anyone older had to remain with their caretakers. Soldiers guided us onto small schooners for an overnight voyage across the Adriatic Sea. Like the cells of one huge being, we adhered to one another and tried to get through this journey as we left the area of Yugoslavia occupied by the partisans.

March, 1944 Santa Croce

Leon, second row, second from left and Sarinka,
stooping in front of him, first row, left.

With no identification papers, we boarded each assigned boat, sat out in the open air with no sanitary facilities and tried to prepare ourselves. Sailing into the chilly night, we crossed over the frigid water chaperoned by a luminous moon, which only increased the risk of enemy detection. I sat terrified, shivering from cold and fear as vast as the body of water we crossed. The moist wind penetrated bone deep. We huddled together and sat quietly as my thoughts wandered to a place too horrible to share. With heaviness in my heart and tears in my eyes, I left my homeland, wondering if I would ever return. I sat traumatized, thinking when—or even more difficult to imagine—*if* I would ever see my mother again, in total disbelief that this was really happening. It was at this camp that we all began to cope with the enormity of our loss, but we were also able to relax for the first time in quite awhile. The goal was for us to be there only a short time.

The next stop was Bari, also on the coast of Italy, probably the safest place for refugees in all of Europe. We hoped we could stay there until the war was over and then go back to Yugoslavia, but we wondered when that would ever happen.

If I'd thought conditions were bleak before, things were even worse in Bari. Upon arrival, we were led to a displaced person's camp with Jews from all different countries. We were given bread and more Spam. Many couldn't handle it and got sick. We were given some medical attention.

Then the men and women were separated. Leon tried to calm me down before they separated us, but I was so despondent at this point that I didn't respond to him. I simply went through the motions, like it wasn't happening to me. We were stripped, and sprayed with DDT for lice. Clothes were redistributed. Approximately seventy people were packed into one room, again with straw-lined burlap bunk beds—only this time there were two on top and two on the bottom.

With scant food and unsanitary conditions developing, the fatigued US military struggled to deal with Yugoslavian refugees pouring into Italy, about 1,800 a week. British soldiers supervised this camp that had already been liberated by American troops, and they were good to us. Soon we became known as a "refugee problem." We recognized some familiar faces from Yugoslavia and we quickly became a tight group helping each other survive.

One day when we were taking a walk I quietly said to Leon, "Look! Doesn't that woman over there remind you of Saphira?" Leon squinted and strained to see. He welcomed even a glimpse of someone resembling his sister. He didn't respond. He said her name softly, and then began repeating it. All of a sudden he broke into a sprint towards the woman. As he got closer, he started screaming her name, "Saphira! Saphira! Saphira!" She turned to look and ran towards him, both with arms outstretched. I stood there motionless with my hands over my mouth.

They hugged, they wept, and held each other like they would never let go. Finally, they sat and cried together as they told each other all they had experienced.

Leon tentatively asked, "Hear anything about Isaac? I saw him in the labor camp and he slipped me a note telling me to get out of there.

"I heard someone warned him he was on the list to be killed the next day so he took the wagon under the pretense of getting food for the people in the camp and never came back. You know Isaac! Given the choice, he would sooner die on the lam rather than sit around and wait. He had the help of a young Catholic woman, Vikića. The last she heard, he was still alive in the mountains with Tito's army."

Leon shook his head as he listened to Saphira and with a wistful smile all he could say was, "At least we know he's alive. Thank God."

Saphira continued, "We decided to go to *Eretz Yisrael*, our Holy Land. It was a big decision for us, but my husband and I decided we want to raise our two sons there. After all that we have been through here it is time to go to our homeland."

Leon's only response was, "We will pray that you will all make this dangerous journey unharmed."

I knew a big part of Leon wanted to join her. When we arrived in Italy we began to discuss possible options and wanted to be ready in case we had to make a quick decision. Leon was deeply afraid of the uncertainty *Eretz Yisrael* still held in 1944, and felt more secure with our final decision to try to get to the United States, if given a choice. I watched sadly as he held his sister. We all embraced knowing we might never see each other again. Our tears of joy became tears of a painful goodbye, but seeing her alive was an amazing blessing. It brought such happiness to Leon, although only for a fleeting time.

Sobbing, Saphira asked, "Do you think Mama is alive? Will we ever see her again? Will I ever see you again?" Not expecting a response she quickly followed with, "Please, please be safe, Leon."

Leon tried his best to be strong for his sister as he held back his tears. I knew he couldn't speak, because if he opened his mouth he would have lost all control. He always tried so hard to be a rock for all of us. Leon just hugged Saphira, eyes welled up with tears, and I heard him whisper a prayer, because that's what he did when things got too tough for him to handle alone.

Part Four

Leon

Isaac Kabiljo, first on the right, standing with other Partisans

Chapter 11

June 9, 1944

President Franklin Delano Roosevelt acted by executive order and invited a group of 1000 refugees to visit the United States. He sent a cablegram to Ambassador Robert Murphy in Algiers stating the following:

Accordingly, I have decided that approximately 1,000 refugees should be immediately brought from Italy to this country, to be placed in an Emergency Refugee Shelter to be established as Fort Ontario near Oswego, New York, where under appropriate security restrictions they will remain for the duration of the war. These refugees will be brought into this country outsideof the regular immigration procedure just as civilian internees from Latin American countries and prisoners of war have been brought here. The Emergency Refugee Shelter will be equipped to take good care of these people. It is contemplated that at the end of the war they will be returned to their homelands.[1]

At the time of this announcement, Sarinka and I had been living in Bari for three months. Like thousands of others persecuted in Europe, this southern Italian city had become a temporary asylum for us, but the facilities housing us were seriously overtaxed. We felt safe there and would

---

1 Franklin D. Roosevelt: "Cablegram to Ambassador Robert Murphy in Algiers on Bringing Refugees to the United States." June 9, 1944. Online by Gerhard Peters and John T. Woolley, The American Presidency Project. http://www.presidency.ucsb.edu/ws/?pid=16519. Special consideration.

have been happy to stay put until the war was over, but was this another miracle?

President Roosevelt's decision instantly became everyone's favorite topic of conversation. We heard it would only be for those refugees with no other haven available. Word spread and people made their way to the American consulate doors all hours of the day and night. Men and women shed tears openly. Some collapsed from the sheer intensity of their emotions. Some held their babies up high for the consulate officials to see, hoping to gain extra consideration.[2]

But I wasn't like that. Somehow I managed to stay calm, even at the most critical of times. As soon as I heard the news officially announced in the camp, I immediately inquired as to how Sarinka and I could be chosen for this opportunity.

With so many vying for inclusion, the chances of getting on this ship bound for New York seemed quite slim. If it were up to Sarinka we would have just stayed put and waited. She'd already left her mother, her hometown, and her country. To go thousands of miles farther away from Europe was not something she wanted to do. She felt anxious and scared. Sarinka trembled just thinking about boarding the ship but she also knew down deep that we needed to save ourselves.

It frightened us both. How could we flee to a country about which we knew so little? We did not speak the language or know their customs. We had no idea what the people would be like, and most worrisome, we didn't know one soul there. Who could we turn to if we needed help? The whole venture terrified us, but I knew we had to apply and worry about everything else later. We still agreed if we were chosen for this ship bound for America, we would go.

The war was far from over and getting away now would be a blessing.

---

2 Michal Eisikowitz/Mishpacha Magazine, Family First Issue 465.

Although it wasn't what we truly wanted, I knew I had to take charge. I went ahead and filled out the application papers.

July 15, 1944

We all heard rumblings about a young woman who was coming from America to accompany the lucky ones chosen. Little by little we learned her name and her story. Dr. Ruth Gruber—a thirty-two-year-old female photojournalist, and a multilingual assistant to Secretary of Interior Harold L. Ickes fought for the assignment to escort 1,000 refugees to Fort Ontario Emergency Refugee Shelter.

This news spread quickly. President Roosevelt agreed to send her on this controversial mission as a "general" for protection in case the Nazis captured her. As a civilian, she could have been accused of spying and therefore killed, but as an officer she would have to be kept alive, protected by the Geneva Convention.

With Ruth's arrival, The War Refugee Board posted the President's cables, which were translated into twelve languages for all the refugees to read. In order to be accepted, however, each family had to sign the following agreement that was translated from English only to French, Italian, and German:

> I declare that I have fully understood the following conditions of the offer of the United States Government and that I have accepted them:
>
> A. 1. I shall be brought to a reception center in Fort Ontario in the State of New York, where I shall remain as a guest of the United States until the end of the war. Then I must return to my homeland.
>
> A. 2. There I shall live under the restrictions imposed by the American security officials.

A. 3. No promise of any kind was given to me, either in regard to a possibility of working or permission to work outside the reception center, or in regard to the possibility of remaining in the United States after the war.

B. 1. I declare further, since I cannot take along any valuta under existing laws, that I shall accept in exchange for my valuta the same amount of dollars, which the authorities of the United States will eventually pay me after my arrival in America.[3]

I read it and tried my best to interpret what this would mean for us. Fortunately, I was quite fluent in Italian. We understood the term "guests of the United States," but it was surrounded by other words that made us question our understanding of the agreement. It seemed to me they were offering us safety and the necessities to live with no other promises. We understood we would be returned to Yugoslavia at the end of the war. I, personally, couldn't imagine what we would return to after all we had heard. We comprehended that we had to live under certain restrictions "imposed by the American security officials" and we knew we couldn't work outside the camp. We had to give up what little money we managed to still have, but in exchange we were promised we would be given that dollar amount after we arrived in America. I wondered if all of this would really be enforced. We weren't the only ones who didn't fully comprehend what we were signing, but what choice did any of us have?

I filled out the application, jumping at the chance to be the first to obtain the necessary forms for us. I heard they did not want to take younger people without children. Not sure what prompted me, I decided to make myself ten years older. I could easily pass for forty-seven due to my premature gray hair. I prayed this would help us in the selection process.

---

3 Lowenstein, Sharon R. Token Refuge, The Story of the Jewish Refugee Shelter at Oswego 1944-1946.Bloomington: Indiana University Press, 1986, page 43. "Departure for the United States of America" (unsigned and undated), Box 2331, Records of the Department of Interior, Office of the Secretary, RG 48, NA.

Sarinka was much less confident about this decision. I tried to convince her this was not only the right thing to do, but our only choice. Still, she was deeply troubled. With love and gentle coaxing, Sarinka knew I only wanted what was best for us. We both agreed to sign the agreement. The problem was the other 3,000 refugees from 18 different countries who also applied for the 1,000 spots.

The more we learned about Ruth Gruber, the more we loved her. When Ruth heard that 3,000 refugees applied we heard she was furious knowing it could have been possible to bring all of them to the United States. She felt 2,000 more lives could have been saved, but President Roosevelt himself announced only 1,000 would be allowed to board this ship to safety. Despite her frustration, we knew Ruth tried to see the glass as half-full from her actions. Everyone paid attention to anything Ruth said and it quickly spread around the camp. We were now getting a feel for who this woman was, especially when we found out she said, "In Hungary, Jews were being selected for death. In southern Italy, a precious few were being selected for life." She knew the most profound part of this mission was that it was the only effort by the United States to save anyone. Her words were heard and repeated. We came to learn more and more about her. Her mission was clearly, " To open doors. Save lives. Circumvent the holy quotas." We loved her vision and her foresight. Before she left, word had it that she told her boss, "These people coming here— they must be frightened, bewildered, coming to a strange land. Someone needs to fly over and hold their hands." Ruth clearly wanted only the best for the refugees. We didn't know her personally yet, but we could feel her love, hope, and determination.

We heard wonderful stories about this amazing country, America. Surely we wouldn't regret signing this agreement. Anything would have been better than the life we now lived, always running from the Nazis. After all, we wouldn't be prisoners, held against our will. But the language barrier didn't allow us to fully understand what we were getting ourselves into. What were the ramifications of signing? The application assured "only safety, security, and shelter for the duration." I wondered if we would truly find our way back to Yugoslavia so we could find Sarinka's mother. Although Sarinka knew we needed to take this opportunity, she felt nauseous when we applied. *Understandable.*

With 3,000 vying for the spots on the ship, what were the chances that some random American official would choose us to be among the lucky thousand, based on what we wrote on our application? We heard applications were taken from Naples and Rome, as well as Bari.

Who would "play God" now?

Chapter 12

W e didn't know it at the time, but Ruth Gruber would be our liberator. She was an amazing intellectual who had attained her Doctor-
ate of Philosophy at the young age of twenty, the youngest student—female or male—to accomplish this anywhere in the world. Ruth observed
Nazi rallies while studying in Germany. It alerted her to this movement
and made her acutely aware of the situation in Europe. She continued to
pay close attention as the news spread.

Ruth became our advocate as well as our friend. It was as some called
her, "Mother Ruth," who fought to bring us over in the first place and it
was she who in the end demonstrated the power of one.

Ruth, who was fluent in German and Yiddish, helped many understand
all that was entailed with signing the papers, but unfortunately not us.
Sarinka spoke only Serbian, but I knew Italian, Spanish, and Ladino. Neither of us, however, knew Yiddish like most refugees did, putting us at
a distinct disadvantage. As Sephardic Jews, Sarinka and I were direct
descendants of the Jewish people who were expelled from Spain in 1492.
So we embraced a Spanish culture. Ladino was a created Spanish-Hebrew language that was used by Sephardic Jews wherever they settled.
Not nearly as prevalent as Yiddish, Ladino didn't always help us communicate, but with the aid of the multilingual backgrounds of other refugees,
communication barriers began to erode.

We were worried, anxious and tired. My clothes were tattered and Sarinka, now gaunt, wore a dress that had become no more than a *shmata*
(an old ragged garment). Her skin, as pale as natural linen, so different

from the day we met. People cried constantly, and we all looked older than our years.

Captain Lewis Korn, one of three American officers who would accompany the refugees, used the following criteria for selection:

> First, we tried to take people in family groups. Then we chose those in greatest need, and took as many as possible from concentration camps and slave-labor camps. Third, we took no families with contagious or loathsome diseases...
>
> And finally we tried to choose people with a cross-section of skills to make the Emergency Refugee Shelter as self-sustaining as possible.[4]

They ended up with "...doctors, dentists, pharmacists, opticians, artisans, merchants, bookkeepers, tailors, dressmakers, teachers, lawyers, singers, actors, painters, writers, sculptors, engineers, and two rabbis."* We discovered later that the American official charged with choosing among them "went to pieces," and actually said, "I can't go on playing God; how can I choose who's going to live and who's going to die?" but that's exactly what he did.

We fit the criteria and we were selected—truly a blessing from God, as far as I was concerned.

1. We were considered an "elderly" healthy couple, thanks to my inflated age.

2. We had been in a slave-labor camp.

3. I was a bookkeeper.

On hearing of our acceptance, I felt like we had just won the lottery. Sarinka, on the other hand whispered, "I know how lucky we are to have been chosen, but my stomach definitely disagrees."

---

4 Gruber, Ruth. *Haven*. New York: Coward-McCann, Inc., 1983, page 79.

I held her close, "Sarinka, I love you so much. This is unbelievably difficult for me as well, but my dream of living the rest of our lives together is paramount. The vision of us with our own children, a vision of both of us feeling safe and able to live a normal Jewish life again…this is what propels me forward. I am constantly focusing on my future with you. We both have to make it through this so we can be happy together and start a family. That is the first thing I hope we do, as soon as we can. Of course, I'm hoping we will reunite with our families at some point, but to get through this I need to focus on what is meaningful to me in my life and right now that is living the rest of my life with you and our children, God willing…nothing else matters. Please tell me as hard as this is, you will be by my side. I can't do this without you, Sarinka."

Sarinka leaned in, gave me a warm hug, and the confirmation I needed. I knew we would make it.

July 20, 1944

We all cheered when military trucks with the Star of David arrived to transport us from Bari to the ship, instead of the usual British military vehicles. My vision blurred with tears as we approached the lined-up vehicles.

We heard that Ruth Gruber contacted her Israeli friends to arrange for the special vehicles because she knew it would calm our anxieties. Someone cared. Someone tried to rescue us. Someone understood. This made it a little bit easier for Sarinka to force herself to go. Me, I couldn't get on the truck fast enough. After all we had been through, what an amazing feeling of safety to ride in this convoy of "Jewish" trucks that trekked hours through the mountains from Bari to Naples, where an American ship waited for us.

Not all of us were Jewish. We heard that Roosevelt did not want it to be a "Jewish rescue project" but a diverse group, and diverse we were. Embarking on the American Troop Transport ship were 525 men and 457 women: 874 Jews, seventy-three Roman Catholics, twenty-eight Greek Orthodox Serbs and seven Protestants—all boarded hoping and dreaming America would treat us better. We were from 18 different countries and our ages ranged from infant to eighty. The actual composition: 368 Yugoslavs (the largest group), 238 Austrians, 153 Polish, 95 Germans, and 40 Czechs.

When Ruth Gruber questioned why we only totaled 982 instead of 1,000, she was told... that's all who got on the ship, after all was said and done. Some were probably too terrified to leave.

Sarinka's unspoken words seemed to congest her every breath. She held so tightly to my arm that I felt her nails digging into my skin. I watched her force one foot in front of the other as we approached the ship. I could sense unvoiced angsts shouting inside of Sarinka's head and in her silent stream of tears. I knew her well enough to know her heart was breaking at the excruciating reality of leaving, not knowing if we would ever return, and I found my heart breaking as well.

Along with 980 others, we climbed the rope ladder onto this whale of a ship, swallowed whole, hoping to be spit out on a foreign shore.

Away from this ludicrous world that we called home.

But, it was our home.

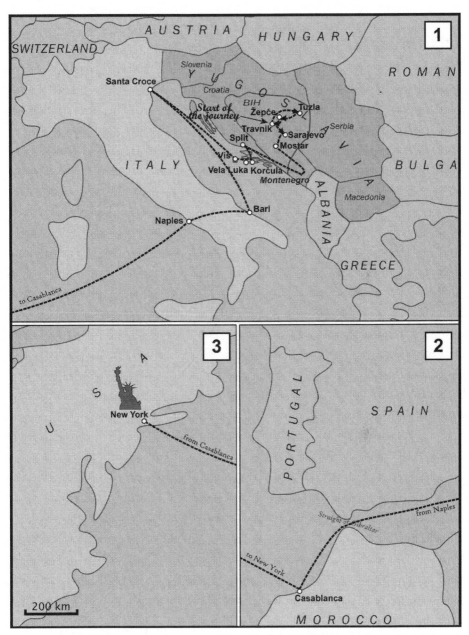

Journey from Travnik, Yugoslavia to America

Part Five

Sarinka

Chapter 13

July 21, 1944
Naples, Italy

We had shared dreadful experiences, and now we shared undesirable close quarters on this voyage. Considered a secret mission, we were never told the name of the ship until much later. The Liberty ship, also known as the *Henry Gibbins*, was not as glamorous as some hoped and envisioned, but it didn't matter. It was the largest ship of the flotilla, carrying 982 lucky refugees and 1,000 wounded soldiers. For us it meant freedom, a word we came to appreciate more than we ever dreamed possible. I knew that deep inside my heart, even though I couldn't show it at the time.

After we boarded what looked like a gigantic warship decked with cranes, ropes and cables, we ran to the rails to say goodbye to our native European countries as we readied to sail across the Mediterranean toward the Atlantic on a beautiful summer day. I watched as we departed with the swell of waves pushing us away from the shore, as my own waves of emotion came over me. Leon saw my eyes fill with tears and kissed me in a moment filled with happiness and sadness for all that we were leaving behind. All of my ambivalent emotions surfaced as I watched the coastline slip farther and farther into the distance. Unlike Leon, who believed this to be another miracle saving our lives, I sat motionless in his embrace, unable to return his hug or join in the jubilation surrounding me. Together we watched the shoreline of Europe for the last time thinking about everything and everyone left behind.

Once I leave, how will I ever get back to Mama? How can I really be leaving her like this without even letting her know? Will I ever see her again?

I closed my eyes. Indelible images I cherished came back to me. I could almost feel the warmth of her skin and imagined her sweet scent when I hugged her goodbye. I could see her beautiful face and the special smile she had when it was meant just for me. *I could easily retrieve these memories now, but what will happen once I get to America?*

I tried to focus on the beauty of the frothy wake glistening in the sun's rays. I took a deep breath of the sea air. I sat mesmerized as tears welled up in my eyes, but not because I marveled at this awesome sight like I did on my summer visits to the shore. No, not this time. This time I was too busy trying to etch this European shoreline and all that went with it in my mind. As I stood there watching this landscape grow dimmer and more distant, I wondered with trepidation how long it would take my memories to fade the same way.

We shared space with the wounded soldiers. We were in the front part of the ship, with the injured in the rear of the same hold. Seeing bandages all over their bodies, I prayed for them to heal when they got proper care back in the United States. In place of the bunk beds we had in the camps, we now had hammocks, three rows high. Our living quarters were terribly hot and many suffered seasickness, but at least our discomfort would be short-lived after a voyage that was supposed to take about ten days. With life in America ahead of us we knew things would be different, and that knowledge empowered us to endure whatever was in store for us over the next couple of weeks.

We ate standing at long counters twice a day. The army could see from our appearance how malnourished we were, and they knew how to feed us. We could not speak English, of course, so we pointed to the food we wanted as the soldiers dished out servings for us. The long loaves of sliced white bread served with jam, and bowls of red wiggly stuff called Jell-O were new for us. They also fed us hot dogs, potatoes, cookies and salads, but best of all was the chocolate the soldiers gave us, a luxury we savored as if it promised sweetness ahead.

The combination of gelatin and seasickness took a toll on me. I was constantly nauseated from eating the red stuff and vowed never to eat it again. Leon found a little burner that they allowed him to use to make tea for me in an effort to settle my stomach. How lucky I was to have such a caring, loving husband.

Berta and Avram Kalderon and their children, Simon and Flora (who we knew from Travnik) were on the boat with us, but we also made new friends, others from Yugoslavia just like us. On the ship, I met Ricki and Silvio Finci and their children Mike and Sonya. Ricki and Sonya walked around clutching a basin in case they vomited from their constant sea-sickness. Since so many didn't have an appetite, those felt fine got back in line two and three times because there was so much extra food—something none of us had seen for years.

After we left Naples in the Mediterranean, we learned that Nazi bomb-ers were searching for convoys like ours because they knew we had sol-diers on the ship. The US sailors put us through daily air-raid drills. Each time I heard the alarm, I tried to suppress my panic. Like a robot I fol-lowed in step with the others as we quickly threw on life jackets and took our assigned positions. With each shrill of the siren my heart raced, as I feared that we were sure to be hit.

At night, the ship tried to become as invisible as possible so that we could move swifter and more secretly than in the daytime hours. No one was allowed out on the decks, no lights were permitted, and the officers had to extinguish their cigarettes. After the third day or so, other ships joined us as we became a convoy of twenty-nine: thirteen war vessels accompanying sixteen cargo and troop ships. Ruth told us the two ships riding beside us were carrying Nazi prisoners of war, who were strategically placed on the outside, like the fenders of a car, to take the first hit if attacked. *Clever Americans.*

Ruth Gruber, however, also had additional thoughts, smarter thoughts. She questioned how they could manage to bring so many Nazi POWs, but only one thousand refugees. She was told the Nazi prisoners would keep the factories and farms working while our men were overseas fighting. This notion did not sit well with her. Ruth knew millions were dying while she struggled to save fewer than a thousand lives. Everyone knew her goal was to rescue as many as possible, and a thousand was not nearly enough for her. But the more immediate concern was whether the thousand of us would even make it to America.

While in the Atlantic, close to Casablanca, Morocco, on our third day at sea, at 2:30 a.m., thirty Nazis planes were sighted flying above us. I knew we had to be prepared, but naively I never believed it would really happen. Leon and I grabbed our life jackets and huddled together in position, perfectly still, whispering our own personal prayers. Once again, we asked God to help us get through this, now that we had come so far.

The commander called for the ship to send out black smoke to hide us as planned, but in all the panic the vents that were supposed to be shut were left open. Smoke filled the lower deck, making many very sick. Unfortunately, the inhalation of the thick smoke hit the soldiers the worst. We could hear them coughing violently and screaming. I shook with fright. Leon held me close, rubbing my back and whispering, "Everything will be okay. It will be okay," though I knew he was just as scared as I was. We trembled together for hours, still in our life jackets. Shots from machine guns suddenly broke the silence. I had no idea if the Nazis were shooting at us or us at them. The explosive boom of the gunfire was like a concussion that struck every inch of my body, reverberating through my ears long after it ended. I cowered, hardly able to hold my head down with my trembling hands. Bullet sounds riddled all of us. Fear assaulted my whole body. I felt numb.

Leon cheered when we heard rumblings that the accompanying warships had protected our ship. The plan worked. The shots fired were at the Nazis, not us. For now, we were safe. No bombs had fallen on us. I overheard some soldiers who thought the Nazis were on their way to a more important mission so they decided not to waste their bombs on the smoky cloud below them. Suddenly, it was silent, with the blackness slowly dissipating, when we heard an announcement to "Stand easy." This had been among the longest forty-five minutes of my life. We survived.

At 3:15 a.m. no one could sleep. The mood elevated to one of joy and laughter for the rest of the night. Now, giddy with relief, the refugees sounded like big shots. Many sat in their bunks and made fun of how easily the Germans had been tricked. I sat in silence, listening.

The next day, the soldiers became more vigilant and practiced their planned drills in preparation for future attacks. The Nazis didn't make us wait long.

The following night at about 1:00 a.m., while tossing and turning, I suddenly tuned in to a silence so startling that it woke me. I heard the ship's engines day in and day out, so the abrupt halt of the constant motor alarmed me. I quickly turned to Leon. "Wake up! Wake up! Something is wrong. Listen to the silence." Just then, we caught sight of Ruth Gruber walking around with her hands to her lips, signaling that no one should make a sound, not a whisper.

What was going on? Would the American soldiers protect us? My heart accelerated as it recognized the danger of this silence.

A submarine attack! I froze, and couldn't move or speak. The German submarine "Unterseeboot," on a mission to find us, heard the hums of the *Henry Gibbins* and the convoy that outlined us as we attempted to sail through the Strait of Gibraltar. Fortunately, with sonar, our ships singled out the din of their engines, just as the Germans probably suspected our presence. Conceivably due to the prudence of Captain John Shea, who commanded the American Troop Transport ship, the silencing of our engines saved our lives as we sat motionless like a corpse in the water. The Nazis did not discover us. Leon continued to fervently believe in our survival.

Our fear of attacks diminished as we sailed farther across the Atlantic and, we hoped, out of range of Nazi surveillance, but, as one might expect, other problems manifested to take fear's place. Asking people from different countries who spoke different languages and practiced different customs to exist in harmony was a difficult challenge. Mistakenly, I thought harmony would be the natural outcome once everyone was on the ship, but instead tensions grew thicker among the different nationalities.

Ruth helped everyone adjust. She provided English classes for us, and even encouraged musical entertainment from the talent among the refugees. Most importantly, she shared her optimistic views for our future. She let us know we were the first to come to America who could share the horror stories we experienced. Although our plight was far from complete, this voyage had brightened the prospects for many.

The Yugoslavs, about a third of the entire group, had suffered a great deal during the war, but it didn't begin for us until 1941. Many joined Tito's Partisans to try to fight back. Although the Nazis invaded Yugoslavia later than other countries, devastating conditions quickly ensued with the help of the *Ustaša*.

We later learned that the *Ustaša* were responsible for the greatest genocide in World War II in proportion to the size of our country. Their leader, Ante Pavelich—a fanatic Croatian fascist with close ties to Mussolini's Fascist Party who hated Serbs and Jews—led the terrorist group with a heinous vision that inspired his followers to brutally butcher and drown

120,000 people from April to June 1941. The *Ustaša* massacres were known to even shock the Nazis. Pavelich told his men, "A good *Ustaša* is he who can use his knife to cut a child from the womb of its mother." We later heard he had a wicker basket on his desk filled with pounds and pounds of eyeballs gouged from *Ustaša* victims. We were told that in August of 1941 Pavelich made a speech that was printed in a local newspaper declaring, "This is now the *Ustaša* and Independent State of Croatia; it must be cleansed of Serbs and Jews. There is no room for any of them here. Not a stone will remain of what once belonged to them."

Hearing some of these stories on the ship made it impossible for me to shut out any thoughts of my family. When it came to the fate of our relatives, I couldn't deal with imagining their specific road to death. The agony of listening to these horror stories grew too much for me to bear.

Consequently, tensions mounted as some Yugoslavs looked down on the German Jews for not having been more defiant, while the German Jews criticized the Yugoslavs for not having suffered to the same extent for as long. The other refugees had no idea what our fellow Yugoslavians were experiencing under the *Ustaša*.

Due to continued language barriers, clear communication remained a challenge. Sometimes, misunderstood words were taken as insults, brewing fights and causing tension that pulsated throughout the ship. I worried what would happen when we all had to live together wherever they were taking us. As usual, Ruth came up with a plan to put out the fires among the refugees, as well as those just starting to smolder between the soldiers and us.

Captain Shea had already warned Ruth the refugees were not allowed to mingle with the soldiers, but Ruth—a maverick in her own way—approached him with another one of her novel ideas. With warranted reason to celebrate and a variety of talent generously sprinkled throughout the group, Ruth boldly suggested the refugees entertain the soldiers. Surprisingly, the Captain agreed to relax the rules and permitted a performance—one he was anxious to see himself.

We heard murmurs among the soldiers. Some were not happy we were there and believed we were endangering them further, causing them to resent us more. I wondered how the soldiers would react to the entertainment Ruth suggested, but I had tremendous confidence in her vision and even I looked forward to the show.

Many talented musicians and singers joined forces to create a variety show filled with music, songs, and humor, filling our time with something productive. Much preparation and excitement went into the program, and it was well worth the effort. The troops showed their appreciation as they laughed, whistled and shouted with the enthusiasm of attending a sporting event, not wanting it to end. With only a few days left at sea, the soldiers finally came to see us as individuals rather than refugees from Hitler with whom they were forced to share their ship.

One day, news spread of a six-month-old baby dying on the ship. We were maybe two days away from reaching America. I couldn't imagine the devastation of these parents who lost Elia, their only child. When I heard the family surname, Montiljo, my heart felt even heavier as that was my maiden name (although they were no relation to me). I was sad and angry at the same time. No baby should have to enter this world in this way, barely given a chance to survive, only to die, weak and vulnerable from pneumonia. This should have been her "Liberty Ship." *How does this happen?* A heaviness prevailed aboard the entire ship. These poor parents suffered the unbearable, agonizing pain of losing their child just one day short of arrival in America. I cried as if she were my own. I didn't know anyone in the family personally, but I couldn't endure this terrible news. Leon tried to console me, but we both knew I was crying not only for this baby, but for so much more. While I was seemingly apathetic on the outside for many weeks, this sadness broke the dam of emotions I had tried to hold back.

Rather than bury Elia at sea, Ruth decided, "She would come to America, the "guest" of President Franklin Roosevelt, to be buried in a graveyard in Oswego."

August 3, 1944

A sight emerged through cloudy skies that I will never forget. Tears of joy I never expected rolled down my cheeks when we came into view of the Statue of Liberty. We all rushed to the ship's rail with the excitement of children pointing, crying, and waving to her and her welcoming torch. Some even kissed the floor of the ship! Approaching lower Manhattan was like seeing a beautiful rainbow break through the clouds after a deadly storm.

Rabbi Mossco Tzechoval approached Ruth Gruber asking her approval for him to lead a special Hebrew blessing that Jewish people say when they wish to give thanks for arriving at a special moment in their lives. This prayer is called the *Shehecheyanu*. The rabbi came forward, bent down and kissed the floor of the ship. After he rose, we all recited it with him. As Leon gently took my hand in his, I said the ancient Hebrew prayer through my tears. From 18 different countries—Yugoslavia, Poland, Germany, Russia, France, Greece, Spain, Hungary, Italy and more— we all chanted the Hebrew words as one:

Ba-ruch A-tah A-do-noi E-loi-hei-nu
Me-lech ha-o-lam she-he-chee-ya-nu v'ki-yi-ma-nu
vi-hi-gi-ya-nu liz-man ha-zeh.

(Blessed are You, Lord our God, King of the
Universe, who has granted us life, sustained us and
enabled us to reach this occasion.)

Then the Rabbi said, "We must never believe the things the Nazis said about us—that we brought evil upon the earth. We did not bring evil upon the earth. Wherever we wandered, we brought the blessings of the Torah. The countries that have tried to destroy us have brought evil upon themselves. As we enter America, remember we are one people. We must speak with one voice, with one heart. We must not live with hatred. We must live with love."

Then he stretched his hands over us with his two thumbs touching in a V formation, separating his fingers to leave spaces only between his thumb and index finger, and middle and ring finger, creating the Five "windows" through which God's blessings could flow, and he recited in Hebrew the priestly blessing. I sobbed breathlessly as I let his words touch my soul, remembering how my father prayed over me as a child.

[May] Adonai bless you, and guard you –

יְבָרֶכְךָ, הוֹהי, וְיִשְׁמְרֶ֒ךָ

(*Yevhārēkh-khā Adhōnāy veyishmerēkhā* ...)

[May] Adonai make His face shine unto you, and be gracious to you –

יָאֵר, הוֹהי יָנָפ וְיִחֻנֶּךָּ

("*Yā'ēr Adhōnāy pānāw ēlekhā viḥunnékkā* ...")

[May] Adonai lift up His face unto you, and grant you peace –

יִשָּׂא, הוֹהי יָנָפ וְיָשֵׂם לְךָ שָׁלוֹם

("*Yissā Adhōnāy pānāw ēlekhā viyāsēm lekhā shālōm.*")

Then he added, "*And may God bless this new land.*" Many wept softly at that powerful moment and all together we said, "*Amen.*"

Ruth began to share what she knew about Emma Lazarus, a Jewish woman born in New York, whose ancestry went back to Spain, as did mine. Emma heard of the mistreatment of Russian Jews and responded with her famous words, written in the 1800s and inscribed on the base of the Statue of Liberty. Ruth recited these most apropos words from memory:

Give me your tired, your poor,
Your huddled masses yearning to breathe free,
The wretched refuse of your teeming shore,
Send these, the homeless, tempest-tossed, to me:
I lift my lamp beside the golden door.

I tried to take it all in as I gazed at my first site of the New York city skyline, emotional on so many levels, watching as we tied up at Pier 84. I smiled with guilty pleasure and diverted Leon's attention to the patina on a green shed I noticed with an old sign that read, "Hamburg-America Line." How ironic that we pulled into a pier that a German firm previously owned?

The soaring buildings, the din of the city traffic and the scents in the air were new to me. With a clear waft of the salt air blowing from the Atlantic, the hot, humid air also brought unfamiliar odors I didn't expect. I took in fetid whiffs of garbage in the Hudson River, and even the newly identifiable smell of hot dogs from nearby food stands. An awesome feeling overwhelmed me the moment I heard the United States Army Band play "God Bless America" somewhere off in the distance on the dock. Tears of happiness overflowed as this great country welcomed us.

We entered the United States of America an exhausted, ragged group. We were a mess, physically and emotionally, not just from our war experiences, but also from the constant seasickness so many had endured. Instead of wondering whether this was all worth it, I had a new sense of excitement and anticipation about life. I already felt welcome—the running was finally over. Looking around me, I noticed I wasn't the only one affected this way. People were suddenly smiling, waving with an exuberance they didn't even know they had in them. At that defining moment, it was as if life went from black and white to color, giving me renewed hope.

A Red Cross boat pulled up beside our ship and women happily handed out sandwiches, doughnuts, cookies, coffee and drinks. A military band entertained us with upbeat songs.

I watched the wounded soldiers and the medical staff as they left the ship. We had orders to sleep on the ship that night.

"Tomorrow the process would begin," we were told.

And what would that process be?

Chapter 14

R uth Gruber left to show her parents that she had made it back alive, but she promised to return to the camp. Since she was our only advocate, it was frightening not to have her there to protect us. I admired and respected everything I knew about this special woman, well aware that we owed her our lives.

We slept comfortably because we felt safe for the first time in more than three years. We awoke the next morning excited—excited that we were in America now, the land of the free! With the war not yet over, we embraced the protection.

Lt. Commander Joshua L. Goldberg, Jewish Chaplain of the United States Navy, helped with the debarkation, assisted by military police and security representatives of the Army, Navy and Coast Guard.

Then it began. Shouted orders told us to disembark so the intake process could begin. To our surprise, aggressive photographers almost rammed their cameras in our faces, and journalists shouted questions so quickly we couldn't possibly have understood them. I think all of us wanted to dodge this brash welcome, but we straggled in, trying to ignore the tumult.

I walked along the dock as my heightened senses exploded again. My skin met the humid heat of New York in August. The smell of coal smoke, manure from the streets, and damp debris were in the air. Men were selling something from pushcarts in the distance.

We were taken along the pier to a *Quonset hut*, a temporary, light-weight, semi-circular structure used by the Navy because they could be set up anywhere and were easily assembled during the war for many different purposes.

First order: Men and women will be separated.

I looked at Leon who saw the horror on my face. This time I was far more cognizant than when we arrived in Bari. He tried to comfort me. "Sarinka, don't worry. I'm sure it will only be a short while. We probably just have to fill out some entrance papers. Please, just follow their directions and try to stay calm. We'll meet up as soon as it's over, I'm sure."

"No, I am not so sure. I can't go through this alone. Please do something!" I cried. While on the ship we had heard many horror stories about the separation done in the camps and it sounded a little too familiar. There were soldiers, no reassuring explanations, and Ruth wasn't back yet. I wasn't the only one terrified by this order.

Leon interrupted my thoughts and took me by the shoulders, "Look, we've come this far. There is nothing we can do now but trust the Americans. You know Ruth wouldn't have left us if she thought something bad was going to happen. You trust her, don't you?"

"You know I do, but I've had you by my side throughout this whole thing. I'm too scared to leave you. I've already left everyone and everything. I can't be separated from you. Please, please don't make me do this. I can't. I can't," I softly sobbed.

Leon responded firmly this time. "Sarinka, I'm afraid you must do this without me. Please do whatever they ask of you. Keep in mind they are trying to help us. I will find you as soon possible."

I suddenly remembered an odd expression my mother used to say to me. *"Sarinka, you won't always be the first hole in the trumpet."* She always knew things would be more difficult for me to handle when I grew up and went out into the real world. She knew I wasn't as resilient as most because of my privileged childhood, and she was probably right.

I tried to reassure myself. *This can't be worse than arriving in Bari, the slave labor camps, or living in the woods among the partisans with the threat of the Nazis at our every turn.*

I unwillingly followed the other women. As soon as we walked into the hut, the next command came.

Second order: Strip naked.

Oh my God! In front of the soldiers? I resentfully removed my clothes, all of them. I covered my private parts with my hands the best I could and ran to try to hide behind others. The muscles of my queasy stomach rebelled as I stood trembling among the women who stood like shivering trees, void of color.

Hoping not to vomit now on top of everything else.

This was what Leon meant when he said I would have to do whatever they asked of me? How humiliating! Would the United States also treat us like animals?

I needed to talk myself through whatever this process was without breaking down. I heard Leon's reassuring words in my head. *"... A short separation . . . Probably for safety reasons . . . This entrance process will hopefully be worth it in the end."*

It was an entrance process all right—disinfestation. I heard screams throughout, my own the loudest. We paraded in front of the soldiers as they deloused our bodies, spraying DDT from top to bottom, giving our private parts an extra spray to be sure we were free of lice and other insects we may have brought into this country. They then examined our heads. I was one of the lucky few with no lice, protected by my thick curly hair. Some had to have their hair shaved. Vaccinations were given. After disinfecting our clothes in a chemical chamber, many of the few possessions we owned shrunk, burned, and/or tore in this process. Clinging to whatever dignity I had left, I salvaged the clothes I could. Then I was handed a tag to put around my neck that read, "U.S. Army Casual Baggage" with an assigned number that I refused to commit to memory.

After they released me, I scanned the crowd looking for Leon. I spotted his silver hair as he too was searching for me. Shouting his name, I ran towards him. As soon as he heard my voice he spun around and ran in my direction. I burst into tears as soon as I felt his comforting touch. I cried telling him the whole experience, but all he said was, "It's over now. It's all over. I know how humiliating it was because I had to do the same, but we did it and we are safe now. I'm proud of you, Sarinka. I can't imagine how tough it was for you to go through that alone." I sat there, unable to say a word, embraced in his curative hug, because that's what I needed to recuperate.

And there was Ruth! Seeing her even from a distance consoled me. True to her word, she returned in time to escort us in to the camp after a visit with her parents and a restful night's sleep.

Friday, August 4th, army soldiers herded us to a ferry that took us across the Hudson River to Hoboken, New Jersey, where we disembarked from the ferry terminal. Now nighttime, they took us to board a special train. The mere sight of everyone packing into the train was all too familiar. Ruth and her assistants wandered through the crowd trying to calm our fears, but you could see the anxiety on our faces. I clearly wasn't the only one who immediately connected this to the horror stories of the European train endpoints, but at least Leon was by my side. Some were all alone and full of apprehension.

Our destination: Oswego, New York. As we rode the train, I invented the worse case scenarios to fill the void in my mind. *How could they treat us like this? Didn't they have any idea what we've already been through? This whole "process" was frighteningly familiar and packing us into this train didn't help. Where to now? What else would we endure?*

August 5, 1944

Riding the train all night gave me plenty of time for pensive thoughts. Nothing could have prepared me for my first view of Fort Ontario when we finally arrived in the morning. I gasped at the sight of six-foot chain link fence, topped with several rows of barbed wire. Others visibly recoiled in fear at the sight. More than half of the refugees on the ship had successfully run from the Nazis, avoiding any kind of concentration camp. Now we arrived at what looked just like the very camps we fought to avoid.

This was America? We had been running like a train with no schedule for years and now we finally arrived at our final destination, only to be welcomed with barbed wire and apparent loss of all freedom? Oh no! Not again! Is this how America would treat its "guests?"

"This site is an old army post. All army camps in America have fences," Ruth reassured us as she tried to reduce the apprehension she read on our worried faces. We were very thankful she was there to assist as we settled into our new surroundings. We needed her comfort to help us ease into this, but we also knew she had to leave in a few days to report to Washington.

Leon noticed my worried expression. "Maybe we should just be happy the enemy is across the ocean this time…no bombs anymore." He was one of the few who immediately looked at it as America trying to keep us safe, and thankfully his optimism redirected my negative thoughts.

Then I overheard a woman saying through her tears, "What is this, another concentration camp?"

And another, "We are victims, why would we be behind barbed wire?"

A man yelled, "How could they do this to us? What do they think we are, animals in a cage?"

I heard other mutterings of protest. I shot Leon a terrified look, but without saying a word his intense eyes told me to keep on moving.

Speechless, I trailed in from the side entrance of the train station directly into the camp, hearing the clicking of cameras from numerous photographers who tried to capture us: weary and forlorn, unshaven and unkempt with soiled tattered clothing, and some poor souls among us didn't even have shoes on their feet. As we entered the camp, an Army official checked us off a master list. Custom representatives inspected our baggage. Guides and interpreters directed us to barracks and mess halls. We were officially turned over to the War Relocation Authority.

My eyes scanned the eighty-acre camp that sprawled from Oswego to the shores of Lake Ontario. White wooden barracks lined up like soldiers. Then, as I walked up a hill, my panoramic view broadened to include the lake waters. Reminded of the seaside of my earlier carefree days, I surprised myself as a smile filled with hope emerged.

Leon's optimism had begun to rub off on me. Now I thought more positively about our situation, appreciating that at least we were safe. It may have looked like a concentration camp, but I knew it wasn't one, and that was a big difference. I had confidence and faith in Ruth Gruber, and I knew she only wanted to help us—to help us survive the emotional and physical trauma we all endured. This would be the only effort of its kind the United States made to save any of us.

Some had relatives who traveled to meet them, but after we were inside the camp they were only allowed to converse through the holes in the fence. We weren't that lucky. We knew absolutely no one. Many Oswego natives stared through the barrier curiously, some leery of us, like we were aliens who'd invaded their community. I guess we were.

Local Jewish and Christian organizations sent translators to help the army with the first few chaotic days. Special forms sent to the camp to secure our personal information were immediately delivered to the National Refugee Service Migration Department (NRS) to help locate any family we may have in the USA. The NRS also provided newspapers, periodicals and books in different foreign languages for a camp library. From Oswego, as well as Rochester, and Syracuse, different groups of people offered musical instruments, shoe repair equipment, and barber chairs. Yes, change was in the air, and some were welcoming us. It felt good.

Joe Smart, the director of the camp, greeted us, shook our hands and consoled us, saying, "When there's a knock on your door, it will be a friendly one." Then we were taken to mess halls and served foods that we were still unaccustomed to: the same sliced white bread we were introduced to on the ship, peanut butter, coffee, milk, hard-boiled eggs, and boxes of cereal—but now we savored this welcomed bounty.

Army personnel screened us with simple questions: Name? Marital status? Children? Country? When asked my name I knew this was the time not to say, "Sarinka." I often thought about what name I would give myself while on this voyage and decided that if and when I reached America I would consciously decide on a new name. Although I recognized this was a temporary residence, I would start now showing my gratitude, trying to assimilate into American culture as best I could without ever losing my Jewish identity. This was a good sign for me to try to move forward now that we were really here. Sarinka reminded me of the country that betrayed me, the country that forced me to leave my mother, the country where friends turned against me. It left a very bitter taste.

Slowly the realization that we may never return to Yugoslavia percolated inside of me. Perhaps that's why I felt so nauseous about this final decision to board the ship. By August 1944, we already heard devastating stories from the other Yugoslavs on the ship. Things sounded grim and it already sounded like our house would certainly not be waiting there for us. We heard that out of 80,000 Yugoslav Jews, the Nazis had already killed 66,000. I refused to give up hope for my family, but the stories we heard crushed my spirit. Preparing myself mentally for what we would come to find out after the war weighed heavily on me. I would never give up looking for my mother, but I began to imagine Leon and I staying in America and our family coming to America to live with us. I did not forget, however, that we were being held at this refugee camp until the war was over and then supposedly we would be sent back, if all went as the United States officials planned it. I could still dream, though.

But for now, for my sanity, I needed to start this new life with a new name, just as in the Bible, where Sarai and Abram are given a new name by God after he speaks to them: "Go forth from your native land and from your father's house to the land that I will show you." Their names were changed to Sarah and Abraham, adding the letter "H" (Hebrew letter "Chai" which symbolizes God's name and life). I, too, would add a letter "H" in what would be my new defining moment. I prayed that adding a lefrom God's name would give me the sense of protection Leon seemed to have. Yes, in this new land I would be known as *Shary,* an American.

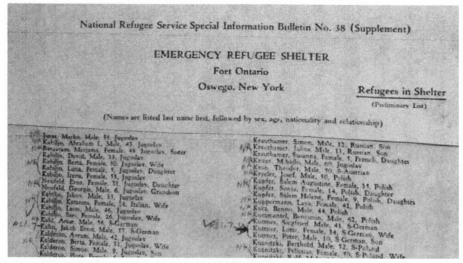

Kabiljo, Leon, Male, 46 Jugoslav—Take note that Leon's age is 10 years older than his actual age. Kabiljo, Seri (Misspelling of Shary) Female, 26 Jugoslav, Wife

SPECIAL INFORMATION BULLETIN

No. 38

August 7, 1944

EMERGENCY REFUGEE SHELTER

FORT ONTARIO

OSWEGO, NEW YORK

Temporary sanctuary for the duration of the war has been provided for 987 refugees who are now in Fort Ontario at Oswego, New York. The group representing 14 different nationalities disembarked at Hoboken, New Jersey on Friday, August 4th. With completion of certain entrance formalities they were placed on a special train Friday night and arrived in Oswego Saturday morning.

Lt. Commander Joshua L. Goldberg, Chaplain, USN, aided WRA at the point of debarkation. Military police and security representatives of the Army, Navy and Coast Guard participated in the handling of the group. Two pullman cars were made available for the aged, women and children.

Names of the refugees in the group are appended to this issue of the SIB. Local refugee committees and family agencies are asked to publicize the list immediately as a means of locating relatives and friends of the refugees in the Shelter. Their names and addresses should be transmitted immediately to the NRS Migration Department.

NRS has sent special forms to the Shelter as a means of securing from the refugees pertinent data concerning their relatives in this country. The forms will be returned to NRS by the camp authorities and NRS will communicate the information thus received directly to its correspondents in all local communities. This procedure is intended as a supplement, however, to such information as the local committees and agencies may obtain through publicizing the lists.

In addition to the services described in SIB #37, NRS will provide foreign language newspapers, periodicals and books for the camp library. Through its cooperating committees in Oswego, Rochester and Syracuse, it will undertake to obtain musical instruments, shoe repair equipment and barber chairs for use in the camp.

Letters to refugees in the Shelter should be addressed as follows:

> Emergency Refugee Shelter
> Fort Ontario
> Oswego, New York

Refugees in the camp will be permitted to carry on correspondence with friends and relatives.

NATIONAL REFUGEE SERVICE, INC. • • • 139 Centre Street, New York 13, N. Y.

Barracks at Fort Ontario (Safe Haven) that housed the refugees
(Courtesy of Sonnenfield Collection; Beit Hatfusot Museum, Israel)

Chapter 15

Escorted to what would be our residence for what turned out to be the next year and a half, we were surprised to see our names already posted on the door. What may have seemed like an insignificant detail to most, spoke volumes to us. After running and hiding for more than three years, we finally had a place of our own. Surprisingly it was a fort that had been in use for two centuries.

The government selected Fort Ontario in Oswego, New York, a former Army camp, for the emergency refugee shelter, later known as "Safe Haven." Since it had closed about three months earlier, it was now vacant and available. They transformed two-story wooden barracks into four small apartments on each floor, separated only by board partitions. We had one bedroom and a small kitchen. Simply furnished in Army décor, our very clean apartment contained two cots, a table, two chairs and a small locker. Not everyone was so fortunate. Some had only beds and needed to wait months for more fixtures to be built. Overjoyed at having this much, we looked at the mattresses and sheets as comforts we'd done without for a long time. Happy tears spilled over as my eyes scanned our small one-bedroom apartment.

The Army soldiers treated us with kindness, giving us chocolate and chewing gum as an extra delight. We went to the dining hall for our first breakfast, where we were served milk and eggs. We were told breakfast would be nothing special, but they had no idea what we lived on for the past few years. Some of the mothers had to remind their children not to gorge so they didn't make themselves sick. They even allowed us to take some leftover food back to our barracks for snacks later. After what we had all been through, this was nothing short of miraculous.

There were communal showers and toilets for males on one floor, females on the other. We were thrilled to hear that the National Council of Jewish Women provided shower partitions and even curtains for our windows to try to provide the privacy deprived of us for so long. When babies were born they donated the crib, layette, infant bathtub, and baby carriage needed. This organization even financed a program for English instruction to benefit anyone interested. ORT and National Refugee Service provided vocational training classes. This was an amazing community. The people of Oswego and the surrounding area donated food, clothes, and even toys—all tossed over the fence. I smiled as I saw how happy Rena Romano (my friend Emma's daughter) was when she caught a doll, remembering how she'd lost her own baby doll before we boarded the ship in Italy. I watched as a teenager on the far side climbed on the shoulders of a friend and somehow carefully managed to get a bike over the tall fence to our side, generously donated by an Oswego family. We were like kids rummaging through the donated items. I found shoes, a decent dress, and other second-hand clothes, all good as new, and now treasures to me.

We received an allowance of $8.50 a month for clothing and incidentals. No one was permitted to go outside the fence to purchase anything in town because of a thirty-day quarantine. Visitors were not permitted in, and we were not allowed out until that time. Uniformed military guarded the gates and censored our mail. Customs agents freely confiscated any packages. Our freedom came with restrictions…still better than from where we came. Not one refugee at the camp emerged from the Nazi scourge unscathed, so it didn't take much to appreciate a place we could now call home, though traumatic experiences still haunted many.

Courtesy of Sonnenfield Collection; Beit Hatfusot Museum, Israel

One night, my screams woke Leon. "What's wrong? It's okay. We're safe now," he comforted.

I sobbed in his arms. "No, No! I had a terrible dream! We thought we were safe at last, but then realized they fooled us and this was really a masqueraded Nazi camp. How do we know it isn't true? My dream seemed so real."

Leon held me. "You just woke from a nightmare. Thank God it was just a dream."

Even though our conditions were improved, fear and paranoia still struck me at times. My thoughts often concentrated on how I would find my mother.

With faith by his side always giving him strength, Leon adjusted more easily than most. A Jewish man from the nearby town of Rochester, New York, brought a Torah, our holy bible, for the camp to use. It didn't need to be hoisted over barbed wire, as it was respectfully delivered to the congregation. Leon was thrilled to hear that Sabbath services would be held the Friday night and Saturday morning following our arrival. We welcomed in the *"Shabbat Bride"* with heartfelt songs that touched our soul. To Leon, having the *Torah* for their first Saturday service was just another miracle proving that his fervent prayers were answered.

Thanks to the Orthodox among us, a Jewish community quickly emerged. With religious services starting the first Shabbat, and more than 200 of us requesting kosher food that followed the dietary laws of Judaism, a kosher kitchen was established within nine days of our arrival. Since Leon was raised Orthodox, this meant a great deal to him.

At last, we had some real privacy, and for the first time in our married life we felt like newlyweds. What we had wasn't luxurious of course, but with food, shelter, and freedom to practice our religion, we began to feel more at peace with ourselves than ever. We could finally sleep a whole night without waking up fearful.

Leon and I were cautiously overjoyed when we learned I was pregnant at the age of 26. A barrage of concerns bombarded my mind. *How would we be able to raise a baby in an internment camp? This is not the way it's supposed to be. No, it wasn't supposed to be this way at all.*

All I could think about was how I wanted to share this news with my mother, but who knows where she was or what she was going through? I started to feel queasy. I needed her now more than ever, and I imagined she probably needed me.

Uncanny how thoughts of both my parents came to me at the most bizarre moments, even though it had been 13 years since my father passed away. I never knew when it would hit me. At times, I managed to live in the present and pushed thoughts of how I left my mother to the back of my mind, but not at this peak moment in my life.

A baby.

A baby growing inside of me.

A baby that came out of our love.

A love strong enough to prevail during these perilous times.

A true miracle.

Even before I got married, I would think about how thrilled Mama would be to hear she was going to be a "Nonna." I couldn't wait to see her face and hear her reaction.

I resented not having the time and space I desperately needed to be alone. I wanted to cry in private when these feelings came over me, and I intentionally kept these thoughts from Leon, not wanting him to worry about me or to diminish his excitement. I should have been so happy, but I never felt as alone as I did then.

Yes, I dwelled on my pregnancy, but I still managed to be right there with the others who not only sought out ways to become useful, but also were eager to begin learning again. Our thirst for knowledge began when Ruth taught us English on the ship, and we begged for more. On our behalf, she went to New York City to meet with leaders from the National Refugee Service. Quickly, teachers were hired to quench our thirst and English was taught to 500 eager adults. By September 5, after a month of quarantine and again with the help of Joe Smart and local Jewish agencies, 189 students from the ages of five to twenty-one in our camp were given an opportunity to attend Oswego's elementary and high schools. The teachers opened up their arms to these children who paid close attention as they spoke in order to best pronounce the new words correctly. Then, the children brought America back into the camp for the rest of us. We all knew that the sooner we achieved an American education the easier our assimilation into this community would be, and we were already hearing stories of prejudice against us. This was when I learned that sometimes you had to have something taken away before you realized how precious it was. After hating school in Yugoslavia, I now understood what a privilege it was to have this second chance in life.

Though the majority of the Oswego residents reacted positively to our arrival, some were leery. We were not surprised to hear of the rumors that we had extravagant apartments with private bathrooms, paid for with their tax dollars. Reports of that nature could only bring animosity, but our leaders realized this meant the people of Oswego needed to get to know and understand us on a more personal level to dissolve the rumors that surfaced.

A "fence club" formed where people from Oswego came to meet us at the fence before the lifted quarantine. For two weeks, curious people of the town came and viewed us through the links as if we were specimens of some kind. As thankful as we were, we realized then that we were still in an internment camp, locked up without true freedom, only this time, not by a cruel enemy.

After the quarantine lifted, Oswego citizens were invited to an open house so they could see for themselves that we did not live in luxury. About 5,000 people came, walked around, and visited our barracks to see first hand how we lived. Hopefully they went back to spread the word and set the story straight.

Months after our arrival in Oswego, an opera was written by two of the survivors before President Truman announced his decision. This appeal for freedom represented the hatred the camp residents felt about their confinement. Sharing their exact words conveys more than I can describe.

I feel myself a monkey
In a zoological garden;
Are we to be on display?

There's nothing missing but the warden!
What are we,—a sensation for tedious people's pleasure?
I can see only prison, not Roosevelt's guests in leisure!

What world are we to live in? What have we then committed?
Are we the foe—the driven? A murderer—outwitted?
We were the cast out people in Hitler's Nazireichen:
Are we the outcasts in highest freedom's nation?

The Golden Cage, Scene 5

The camp officials deprived us of information—something we needed now more than ever. With the war not yet over, we desperately wanted to know the world situation, but we had little contact with those outside the fence. The young adults found a way to deal with the situation using their survival instincts. They dug a hole under the fence, crawled through, and then hitched into town to bring news back to us. Even after the ban was lifted, incoming and outgoing mail was denied until about six weeks later. Yes, we were safe, but we never expected to have news withheld from us when we were in the great United States of America. Shortly after the quarantined ended, we were allowed out on a pass for up to six hours.

Mary Richardson, a wonderful Christian woman, exemplified our personal experience of how welcoming and special the people in the town were. She brought us goodies, but most importantly, she came often, always bringing her care and concern. She immediately connected with Leon and me and welcomed us, out of the goodness of her heart. Although tremendously grateful for Mary's kind friendship, I still felt like a caged animal as the only communication I had with her was through the fence. As time went on, Mary was allowed to take us out with the special six-hour pass, but only if chaperoned by her and with the assurance that she would return us at the proper time. She took us out to lunch and even to her home for a visit. We felt very fortunate knowing that she enjoyed her time with us as much as we did with her. Mary's visits revitalized the hope and excitement we felt when we first laid eyes on the Statue of Liberty.

Oswego, 1944 Sarinka (now Shary), seated, far left
on bench and Leon seated on right

Written on the back of the photo: "Spring 1945 Bar Mitzvah of Mike Kamhi." Leon Kabiljo, is the only man in this photo. All were widows, except for Sarinka, pregnant and sitting in front of him.

November 1944

We didn't have freedom, but we had food, shelter and medical attention. Soon we were all given jobs within the camp like firemen, cooks, etc. Each apartment had its own kitchen so we could cook if we preferred, but three meals a day were provided. The camp had three well-organized kitchens with designated meal times. My good friend Ricki became one of the cooks. She would cook for 100-130 people and she received $18 a month. Her cooking was so scrumptious that she quickly developed a following. Whenever we heard she was the cook, we all flocked to eat her meals.

Luckily, we made friends in the camp who became our family. We even had our own club. Together we read books and learned English. We played cards, did crafts, and basically had no worries.

Things were looking up, but then the harsh weather of upstate New York penetrated our weak souls. Daily snow and consistent gray days depressed many. We were safe, but we were still not totally free, and that was probably the hardest thing for everyone to accept.

December 29, 1944

Shocking and tragic news erupted among us: a young woman in the camp committed suicide. Her name was Karoline Bleier, a thirty-two-year-old beautiful married woman with two babies. This shook each of us to our core. We didn't know her personally, but she was Yugoslavian and a part of all of us.

Later her story surfaced. Those of us who didn't know Karoline well thought she lost her first husband and two children to the Nazis, but that wasn't the case at all. Back in Europe, while married with two children, Karoline fell in love with a man named Geza, and her only thoughts were to be with him. The stakes were high. To divorce her husband, she would be forced to give up her two children, but her sole focus was to be with the man she loved. Karoline married Geza and they had two children together—two-years old and nine-months old at the time of this incident. Those who knew Karoline told us she frequently spoke of her first two children, asking, "Why did I abandon them? If they are dead, I am to blame. I killed them." This plagued her terribly. One late afternoon, she told Geza she would be back soon and asked him to take good care of the children. What he didn't know—and what an autopsy later revealed—was that she swallowed 100 aspirin tablets before she left. Geza, afraid that she became a victim to the terrible snow and wind, begged the searchers not to give up, but to protect their own lives they finally quit late into the night. Searching by the canal the next morning, they found Karoline dead from exposure to the extreme cold.

The mood in the camp began to fall like the temperatures of the unforgiving winter. The dreams we had of coming to America faded with each day. Some of these negative conditions overshadowed the clean bedding, clothes, food and religious freedom we had finally achieved.

Although we were grateful for these amenities, they did not take away our future concerns or the nightmares that haunted so many of us. All that we received at the camp didn't alleviate my own imminent fears of bringing a Jewish child into this community, especially knowing we signed papers saying that we had agreed to go back. Back to what?

Little by little, we discovered disturbing facts. Most ironic was that America had brought in more than 400,000 German POWs into the country, but fewer than 1,000 war-torn refugees. The POWs were paid minimum wage to work in American fields and factories while young American soldiers fought in Europe against Germany. Some of the refugees, yearning for the chance to be productive, requested the opportunity to work outside the camp. Fifty refugees were given permission to work either in the fields or at a nearby Birds Eye factory. Unfortunately, this only lasted for one day. "Bureaucratic problems," we were told.

I later found out how well the Nazis were treated at Fort Niagara, also in New York State. They had access to a library, a variety of sports, movies, and the same diet the American soldiers were fed. They had a school, a newspaper, and even an orchestra! They were given summer and winter clothes and private places to live, in addition to spending money. This was very difficult for all of us to swallow, knowing how the Germans had treated Jews. It made no sense to me.

Despite discovering how the prisoners were treated and other disappointments we dealt with, I still felt grateful for our new surroundings. Wasn't that the most important thing anyway? We were finally in a safe place. Sometimes I had to keep reminding myself of this.

Winter in Oswego, 1945 Shary and Leon on left (Unidentified woman and children)

January 17, 1945

Today we heard that President Roosevelt had written a letter reaffirming his feelings that he "definitely" would like us returned to Europe when it could be safely organized, and until then we were to be restricted to the camp. This was in line with what he assured Congress back on June 12, 1944. We were invited as "guests", but we felt increasingly like prisoners of uncertainty.

February 19, 1945

We thought we were used to severe winters in Travnik, but that was nothing compared to the frigid temperatures we experienced at the camp, with snow and ice all around us. We basically couldn't leave the camp giving us even less contact with the outside world. It was hard to stay warm. Many became even more depressed. We began to feel like a "forgotten village."

This morning Leon left to shovel coal into a truck that would be delivered to heat the furnaces...his work for that day. He expected it to be a normal day, but another tragedy struck. Silvio Finci, one of Leon's best friends, had unexpectedly switched jobs with Arpad Buchler. Even though it was not his turn, Arpad offered to shovel from the ten-foot mound of coal piled out in the open by the camp's main entrance. Silvio would load the truck instead. Arpad was the kind of guy who did everything with a smile. Humming a cheerful tune, he began digging into the mountain of coal. Without warning, huge ridges of ice on the pile that had been melting in the sun came tumbling down on him along with heaps of coal. Everyone rushed over to help him, and they frantically tried to uncover poor Arpad, using any available resource from their spades to their bare hands. They finally got to him and quickly carried him to the campground hospital, but he was already dead.

Leon came home and told me the whole story. Shaken from this tragic event, he also realized this could have been his best friend, Silvio.

"Oh my God! Karoline, and now Arpad? Why? Arpad was so young, married with four little children! He survived the Nazis, and now this! He was so kind, known for his good attitude towards everything and everyone. Why such a pointless death? How can you make sense of this? I can't," I cried.

He tried comforting me as I wept. I was six months pregnant and crashing waves of sadness came crashing down on me. We sat and held each other.

Then we rose and left our apartment to find our friends. We needed to cry and grieve together for yet another senseless death. We did what Jewish families do when tragedies happen. We gathered and sat with his wife and children for the *Shiva* period. We served them meals and we prayed together to help elevate the soul of this righteous man. We all needed these prayers to reaffirm our faith in God at the very time we questioned it the most.

Morale continued to plunged in the camp and our withered souls took a beating. People were feeling more and more isolated. The Yugoslavs stayed in our own group so we had little contact with others. Some expressed envy of those living meaningful lives in the outside world. Leon and I, though, were happy enough with our lot in life at this time. We were more concerned with what would become of us when the camp closed.

Along with my belly, new fears continued to grow.

Chapter 16

April 12, 1945

News of President Roosevelt's death fell on us like a bombshell. We finally had access to a radio in the camp and listened intensely to every detail. His butler had brought him lunch and observed that the president seemed uncomfortable. Then suddenly he cringed, putting his left hand to his head as he said, "I have a terrible headache." Those were his last words. He collapsed into an unconscious state and could not be revived although many attempts were made to save his life. The doctors pronounced him dead at 3:35 p.m. at the age of sixty-three. Vice President Harry Truman arrived at the White House by 5:30 p.m. and within the next hour and a half, Truman was sworn in as America's new president. We wondered what this would mean for us.

I gazed through my tears at the lowering of the American flag to half-mast and listened to the "The Star Spangled Banner" with the others. People sobbed for the man who we only knew as our liberator, the man who sadly didn't live to see the end of the war. Some went to the synagogue to recite *The Mourner's Kaddish*. If Roosevelt had not given his initial approval for 1,000 refugees to be brought to the United States, we would have ended up among the millions of Jewish victims, rather than among the survivors. He was responsible for saving us and now he was dead. We wept and mourned again. This time, we all shared a huge loss.

At the camp, we all listened to Fredi Baum, a young man from Yugoslavia, as he gave a fitting eulogy.

He was a great fearless leader of warm qualities, upon who the whole world focused its attention, to lead it out of barbarism to the light of liberty, freedom and happiness. Though we are not citizens of this country, though most of us have become stateless, we understand perhaps better than any others what this death means to the entire world.

Fredi Baum April 1945

April 28, 1945

Again, we sought out a radio when we heard the murmurs about Benito Mussolini, the Italian dictator and Nazi supporter who led Italy into WWII. We heard a graphic account of how the Italian partisans executed Mussolini, along with his mistress, Clara Pettacci. After their horrible death near Lake Como, the Italian partisans took them to a Milan gas station and hung both by their feet, along with other cohorts, for the world to see. The radio announcer described the anger of the crowd. One woman shot Mussolini's body five times, one for each of her five murdered sons. Others spat on him as they walked past. As I listened, I wondered if this event meant things were finally starting to take a turn in our favor.

April 30, 1945

Then we heard the news we had long hoped and prayed for—Hitler's death. And we wanted to know every detail. Our tradition teaches us not to celebrate the death of an enemy, but one of the most evil men in all of history was finally dead and we wanted to know more.

By April 22, Hitler finally realized that Germany was going to lose the war. On April 29, he married Eva Braun. As the Soviets approached his bunker, he and his wife of forty hours were found dead in his study. We heard that Braun poisoned herself and Hitler shot himself in the head.

Their personal SS bodyguard saturated them with gasoline and set their bodies on fire.

With the tumor responsible for spreading this ravaging cancer finally removed, would we begin to heal from this?

Hard to believe this evil man is gone.

The world would be a safer place.

My baby wouldn't have to grow up in a world that boasted of such a notorious leader.

I could breathe easier.

Thank you, God.

May 7, 1945

The Second World War finally ended in Europe! Germany surrendered. The running and hiding, the senseless torture, the heinous medical experiments, the murders—all over at last. The world would learn what we had been through and the search for our loved ones—or what became of them—could begin. My thoughts were consumed with finding my mother.

"Leon, I'm so thankful. I don't remember when I felt relief like this! There are no words! For the first time in almost nine months, I can honestly say I am thrilled about my pregnancy, knowing our baby will come into a better world. Now, we need to find our families. Maybe they won't hold us to the agreement we signed and we can stay in America. Maybe we can convince them they must come to America too!"

Leon smiled. "I hope it's that easy, Sarinka. We will at least try our best to find everyone. As soon as possible we will write letters to our hometowns and seek help from the Jewish Organization."

This is a great day indeed! Thank God it's over and the Jews can live safely again." He took my hand and joyfully we joined the others.

We assembled outside on the campgrounds to shouts of jubilation. Everyone hugged, laughed, cried, danced, and prayed. Some went to their apartments to be alone to digest the news. The euphoria spread throughout the camp. I rejoiced, hugging Leon with gladness in my heart. This exhilarated feeling was new for me. Can't remember when I felt like this.

May 18, 1945

Now that the war was truly over, Leon and I eased into contentment with the life provided for us, even though we still did not have complete freedom. Some were so plagued with the guilt of surviving that their numbness didn't permit them to feel anything. You could see and hear how depressed many refugees were. Compared to the life of running and hiding since the day of our wedding, Leon and I only had gratitude for our situation. As we waited to see how our future would unfold, however, we also began to feel anxious.

Now with nine months behind us, we eventually took over all the jobs in the camp, although we were still under the supervision of a few hired Americans. Anyone who worked received $18, regardless of the job level. Leon did different kinds of work, which included taking care of the heating system, shoveling coal in to the furnace, cleaning the barracks, and acting as a firefighter when needed. An educated man, versed in Serbian, Spanish, Italian, Ladino, Hebrew, and now learning English, shoveled coal knowing that's what he needed to do at this time in our lives, and he did it without complaint.

We welcomed the spring weather and along with the buds, culture sprouted in our lives. Once again, we could feel comfortable and proud of our Jewish heritage. There were movies a few times a week, concerts, plays, art and poetry classes, folk dancing, and even Boy Scouts for the young ones. Because Leon loved to sing, he joined a choir that formed among the men. This nourished one of his earlier dreams of becoming a cantor, the person who leads A Jewish congregation in melodic prayer. We also played chess and read magazines and books in English.

The National Refugee Service provided some kind of a copy machine for a weekly newspaper, Ontario Chronicle written by those who were surprisingly already proficient in English. Someone in our Yugoslav group thankfully wrote a condensed version in Serbo-Croatian. We were so hungry for information of any kind.

Although we had glimpses of the outside world and these activities helped us seem like a normal community, we knew we still didn't have our freedom. Yes, refugees married, had babies, and even died in the camp, but living in limbo was not easy. Thankfully, Leon's resiliency became my source of comfort.

The fort consisted of five historic buildings around the circular parade grounds inside a thick stonewall, shaped like a star with five protective points that guarded this port. I remember how safe I felt when I walked this area many times in the months waiting for the baby. Usually though, I strolled outside of the fort area and I watched the children play Ping-Pong or racket ball near the barracks.

After Leon left for work I was home alone trying to keep busy. in the morning. That afternoon I felt cramps in my stomach and my back. My friend Berta, who already had two children of her own, stopped by to check on me. "Sarinka, you're probably in labor. We must take the camp bus to the hospital before the pain worsens."

"No, Leon isn't here. I can't go without him. He won't know where I am when he gets home.

"Sarinka, please listen to me. Be reasonable. I know from experience. We can send someone to find Leon and tell him where to meet you. Please, get what you need and let's go!" I obeyed reluctantly as my cramps intensified. I reminded Berta to check me in with my American name Shary after we arrived at the station hospital on the campgrounds.

When I arrived, the nurse confirmed that I was in labor and they prepared me for delivery. Thankfully, someone volunteered to try to find Leon. By the time he arrived, I was experiencing intense labor pains.

Just after midnight on May 19, 1945, my daughter was placed in my arms, swaddled in a pink blanket and adorned with a pink ribbon in her dark hair. Leon stood beside us with a smile and tears in his eyes. Yes, I had tears in my eyes too…tears of happiness, but also wistful with thoughts of my mother, knowing I might never have the opportunity to introduce to her Sylvia Simcha.

Leon indulged me with the selection of our baby's first name: Sylvia, a name I loved, and Simcha, (after Leon's mother, Simha) which means joy. As Sephardic Jews, we decided to honor Leon's mother with her name. We gave this a great deal of thought because Jewish mysticism teaches that the newborn may take on the traits of that person. We could only wish for Sylvia to take on Simha's characteristics, a good-hearted kind person, loved by all who knew her.

With my healthy newborn in my arms and my husband by my side, I experienced a joy I never dreamed possible. I was a mother now and I needed to embrace this new role, but it wasn't so easy. I constantly struggled with the guilt of knowing there were many less fortunate, but that didn't take away the emptiness I felt having neither of my parents to share this joy with me. I was dealing with my own personal reality. Realizing how lucky I was to survive didn't make dealing with the loss of my family less painful. Perhaps Sylvia was the ointment I needed to help my heart heal.

While in the hospital, I met Maria Montiljo, the woman who had lost her baby on the ship, when she was discharged after giving birth to her new daughter, Rosica. I was so happy for her! Of course this baby could never replace Elia, but I witnessed first hand how to continue living in spite of one of the greatest losses of all. Maria pushed herself to continue to try and find happiness again, and watching her gave me strength.

During my two-week stay in the hospital, which was typical after giving birth in the camp, a nurse looked after us. She taught me how to care for my baby because I knew nothing about infant care. With the hospital right on the campgrounds, Leon visited whenever he could and together we embraced this new chapter in our lives, emerging as parents after our traumatic beginning.

One day while still in the hospital, I had a visitor I have never forgotten. Eleanor Roosevelt walked into my room! She came towards me with a smile and spoke in such a friendly manner. As she introduced herself, she shook my hand and then oohed and aahed over Sylvia, held her, and gave her a kiss! I could barely answer her question when she asked, " How do you like America?"

Nervous and self-conscious about my broken English, I answered with a laugh, "So happy for America, Mrs. Roosevelt. Everyone nice. Happy." Word had it that Ruth Gruber invited Mrs. Roosevelt to promote the idea of the refugees staying in the United States. To whatever I owed that delightful surprise, I treasured her visit and on occasion boasted that the former First Lady held my baby!

A nurse came daily for about a week after we were discharged from the hospital to continue to help teach me how to care for Sylvia. Knowing little and having no one at home to help me, I appreciated this assistance and would tell Leon all about my day when he walked in from working whatever daily job he was assigned.

My distant cousin Esthera surprised me with an intimate baby naming party for our newborn. The Rabbi came and said a blessing over Sylvia and announced her Hebrew name, Simcha. How did all our new friends manage to bring her a gift? I received a baby book and other handmade items, but Esthera's surprise was the best! She removed her own beautiful blue Star of David necklace and gently placed it around Sylvia's neck, explaining why she wanted her to have it now. "Sylvia, I hope you'll wear this special necklace and feel the love and the strength of our faith that comes along with it. You represent joy and rebirth to all of us. May God bless you and protect you always." We all sensed the magnitude of this symbolic gesture and I wasn't the only one crying as we listened to Esthera's words. I looked around and felt a loving embrace from all these wonderful people who had become our family and who welcomed our baby into the world. With uncertainty ahead and confinement to the camp, the love we felt at this party gave us hope for Sylvia's future.

Sylvia Simcha brought joy and happiness to all of us. Among the 23 babies born in the camp, she was more than just another newborn. She was a symbol of revival that we all needed to see. She represented the joy we felt starting a new life and she reminded us why we had pushed ourselves to survive.

Leon and I stared at her constantly, unable to believe we now had a precious baby girl, but the feeling of love that surrounded our baby and us that particular day transcended words in any language. I spontaneously smiled from a place so deep—a huge smile, one I thought was lost forever. Softly, I whispered in my native tongue, "Sylvia, welcome to our new world!"

Part Six

Leon

Chapter 17

A mbivalence filled the air. Of course we were thrilled the war was over, but we were also laden with the anxiety of having heard our deportation date was set for June 30, 1945. Rumors of returning us to Europe ran rampant, causing added anguish. The question of what would become of us was one that we all asked—the refugees, the United States government, and the people of Oswego, but I needed the answer to this question for personal reasons. As a husband and father now, I needed to take care of my family.

Ruth Gruber wrote a letter indicating that we were "nearly American-ized" and should be permanently permitted in, as part of our country's immigration quota. "It's time we showed that this administration has a policy of decency, humanity, and conscience and the guts to carry that policy through," she firmly stated. A committee that included Eleanor Roosevelt, Ohio Senator Robert A. Taft and the original director of the camp, Joseph Smart, all worked diligently to help our cause.

On behalf of all of us, with the mayor's direction and more than two dozen prominent citizens of Oswego, President Truman and Congress received a document on May 21. They recognized the contributions we made and would continue to make to American society in the future. The people of Oswego rallied for us. They were desperate for a decision to permit the refugees to remain in the United States but they were well aware that President Truman didn't share this opinion. He knew the refugees signed papers promising President Roosevelt they would return to their countries.

We, the refugees, knew how fortunate we were to be in this particular city, populated with amazing people who realized our virtues and who were not afraid to stand up and fight for us. The teachers in the community who taught our refugee students expressed that they were some of the finest students they ever had. The Syracuse Art Museum recognized their art with exhibits attended by hundreds of visitors due to the students' artistic talents. A group of energetic young adults belonging to an organization known as the Friends Service took quite an interest in the refugees. They taught the children about scavenger and treasure hunts as well as American folk dances. All the refugees more than accepted their help.

May 30, 1945

Only thirteen volunteered to return to Yugoslavia now that the war was over, although more decided at later dates. Seven were single adults, one family of three, and a man whose wife and children joined him the following August.

As far as we knew, Shary (still trying to get used to her American name) and I had nothing left and at this point had no intention of returning. Authorities at the camp helped us investigate our hometowns now that the war had ended. We heard 66,000 Yugoslav Jews were dead—a devastating number. No one knew anything about our families. It was if they had been plucked from this earth with no remains, so we assumed the worst.

Day after day, we continued probing until we sadly learned the probable fate of my mother-in-law and her mother. All the people in Shary's hometown were taken to Jasenovac concentration camp. Non-Jews were living in Jewish homes. That's all we were told.

Shary's search for her mother was now over. All hope expired—hope that was paramount in helping us survive day to day. Now what would help us move forward?

I stared at Shary in disbelief, but she stood silently. I didn't speak. I knew these words pummeled her soul. I thought she might pass out. After the words sunk in, she wept from the depths of her heart. Finally, she spoke through her sobs, repeatedly saying, "No, no. This can't be. Maybe there's still hope. Maybe she's hiding somewhere. Oh my God, please tell me this can't be. No...no...no." I took her in my arms and held her, trying to absorb her heavy sobs.

Soon after it was my turn to have my kishkies torn apart. We heard about my mother, grandmother, four brothers and one of my sisters, all believed to have been murdered at Jasenovac Camp in Yugoslavia. I sat numb, wringing my hands, trying my best to be strong for my wife, but finally the tears came. We just sat and held each other.

Life would never be the same for us. How do we return to normal? How will we love again? This final news shattered our lives. We can't cry anymore...no tears are left.

We were not alone though. Other refugees in the camp heard similar disconcerting news and sadly shared our devastation.

July 3, 1945

Finally, a congressional subcommittee voted on a resolution asking the American government to grant us our freedom. Interestingly, they put the following clause in: "No groups should be brought into the United States under these conditions in the future." *Wait...wasn't America a country that was held to a higher standard than most and rescued those in need? What if, God forbid, a genocide like this ever happened again?* This sounded more political than humanitarian to me but I focused on the fact that the resolution passed. Finally, we received the news we were waiting and hoping to hear. We were told we could walk out of the fenced in area and enter the United States of America...but then what?

July 6, 1945

Three days later, a new development: the House Immigration and Naturalization Committee decided this was not a decision for Congress, but one for the Departments of State and Justice. Dependent on their judgment, we could be declared "illegally present in the country" and they would "undertake deportation proceedings" against us, claiming immigration laws could not be changed. Our jubilation turned to despondency.

We began to realize some of the problems with the Emergency Refugee Shelter. We found out that those who stayed in the camp in Bari and who chose not to get on the ship had freedom months before we did. They surely dealt with their share of problems, but they went back to their countries to start anew. At least it was their country and they knew the customs and the language.

At the camp, with this latest news, we now dealt with frustrations and uncertainty. I could see just from my own observations that there were refugees who actually deteriorated here. Some had episodes of paranoia, and some showed individual and/or social dysfunction. I was glad Sylvia was just a baby so she hopefully wouldn't suffer as some did with their parents not being able to be emotionally available for them during this period. Many of the children depended on their friends for primary support. Our Yugoslav "family", however, formed intense relationships and truly looked after each other, especially the offspring of our group.

We truly didn't know what would become of us and where we would go from here, or if we would ever be allowed to stay in America. If they did change their minds again, how would we survive here? Where would we go? Our comforts had been met for the 14 months we were in the camp. I worried about how I would provide for my wife and daughter now, but I still felt resilient and eager to start anew. *Will I be given the chance after all this?*

After living in America, we were different people than the ones who stepped off the *Henry Gibbins*. We had changed for the better, thanks to the American government and many of its people. We were not dressed in frayed clothes and shoes anymore. We were not totally free, but we were stronger and healthier in so many ways. Many of us had to have our teeth replaced after they'd decayed and rotted from years of forced neglect. Thanks to the government and Jewish agencies dentures were made for us. Some were grateful to receive eyeglasses, artificial limbs, and other medical services they may have needed.

Thanks to good people like Mary Richardson who came to visit us and took us out of the camp, we learned much about American life. We experienced American holidays and customs. We started to dress like Americans, and we could even speak the language now. More than anything, most us of simply yearned to be Americans. We were grateful and longed for immersion into American society and culture. We did not want to look back.

December 5, 1945

The Chairmen of the House and Senate Committees on Immigration and Naturalization received a letter from the Justice and the State Departments advising them to deport us from the United States now that the war had ended. The document was to be signed by Harold L. Ickes, the Secretary of the Interior, Attorney General Tom C. Clark, and the Secretary of State, James. F. Byrnes. But of the three, Ickes refused to sign the letter.

Each update took us up and down an emotional roller coaster. This took a toll on all of us.

December 22, 1945

Again, a brave Interior Department employee, Ruth Gruber, an assistant to Ickes, came to our aid and fought for us to stay in America. Ruth drafted a new letter and we had confidence in her ability to persuade. She knew we had been carefully screened before our selection in Italy. Although sixty-six out of 369 Yugoslavs chose repatriation, Ruth knew the majority of us preferred to stay and were devoted to living in the USA, a democratic country, especially after what we'd experienced. Ruth wrote a letter explaining her reasoning (along with others who wrote in our favor) to Under Secretary of State, Dean Acheson, who would discuss this with President Truman. In the meantime, a congressional delegation arrived and questioned many of us in order to go back with their recommendations for President Truman. We had no idea what to expect.

Ruth called and told us to listen to the radio tonight, as she would do from her own apartment, to hear the outcome of Truman's deliberations in a speech to the nation. She had no idea what he had decided. She shared our apprehension to hear the final outcome of the Second World War when it came to the relatively small group of us refugees...the beneficiaries of the one and only instance the US government went outside the immigration quotas of the day.

We gathered together to listen. No one spoke a word. Looking around I saw familiar faces without smiles, heads hung down, and many wringing their hands. Shary sat biting her nails and swallowing hard, bracing herself for what we were about to hear. How many times had we been through these intensely stressful situations? My anxiety lingered with each extra minute we waited. I worried for my wife and our baby, not knowing where Sylvia would grow up and how she would live her life. The music came to a halt. There was an almost frightening silence. With our English much improved, we clung to every word as Truman began to speak in his even tone.

He began by explaining, "The war has brought in its wake an appalling dislocation of populations in Europe... The immensity of the problem of displaced persons and refugees is almost beyond comprehension."

"... To the extent that our present immigration laws permit..." "...everything possible should be done at once to facilitate the entrance of some of these displaced persons and refugees in the United States."

Between my nerves and my English, I could barely comprehend it all. I heard the president say that the quotas would not change. The laws allowed for 3,900 monthly visas, and this would help the displaced people from the war. I was getting even more tense and worried. It sounded to me like he was not recommending any accommodations to the immigration laws to help us.

Finally, he spoke about our group. Dripping with sweat on this cold December day, I tried to prepare myself for what I was about to hear. Still difficult for me to understand English when spoken quickly, I listened intently to President Truman explain that Roosevelt's plan had been to return us to our native countries after the war. We all knew we'd signed the papers agreeing to that, but so much had changed since then.

Go home? What home?

Now we want to stay here! What in the world were we going to do? How will I provide for my wife and daughter? Where will we live?

Then came the words we waited to hear as he told our unique story:

There is one particular matter involving a relatively small number of aliens. ...However...surveys have revealed that most of the people would be admissible under the immigration laws.

In the circumstances it would be inhumane and wasteful to require these people to go all the way back to Europe merely for the purpose of applying there for immigration visas and returning to the United States.

Many of them have close relatives, including sons and daughters, who are citizens of the United States, and who have served and are serving honorably in the armed forces of our country.

I am therefore directing the Secretary of State and the Attorney General to adjust the immigration status of the members of this group who may wish to stay here, in strict accordance with existing laws and regulations.

Harry S. Truman December 1945

Oh my God! Did I hear that right? Maybe I misunderstood what he said. Do we finally have the freedom we have prayed for?

I looked around. Some gaped as they heard this jaw-dropping news. I continued to scan the room. Heads instantly lifted with eyes wide open! Everyone began to go crazy! They clapped, laughed, kissed, wept, hugged, and jumped up and down! Sounds of triumph! Yes! I had understood him correctly. I hugged and kissed Shary with tears in my eyes. We joined in the pandemonium, hearing cries of joy as people danced around and in unison we all broke into refrain from the *Battle Hymn of the Republic*, singing… *"Glory, Glory Hallelujah."*

This moment defined our lives. We already loved America. Opportunities we never could have dreamt possible while we struggled to stay alive in the woods were now before us. It was so hard to believe! I knew this was divine intervention, and on Shabbat, no less! I continued to pray, thanking God each day.

Chapter 18

New Year's Eve 1945-1946

Excitement permeated the entire camp. The refugees performed the opera, The Golden Cage that had become the saga of our camp lives—from the displaced person's camp in Italy to their camp experience. As time went on some scenes were changed to express how we are still "sitting behind the fence, looking longingly at the Statue of Liberty, singing sadly."

Behind the fence of Fort Ontario
We are sitting, awaiting the glorious day,
When our unchained feet may finally go
Over the most wonderful country's way.

There is no food we are longing for,
No material need we are suffering,
But our hearts have never been cared for,
Are ever tremendously troubled.
Like a lion in the cage
We are losing health and mood;
Like a bird, which after age
Finds its wings for nothing good.

The Golden Cage

Now, however, a newly written conclusion revealed the elation they felt to be truly liberated, taking them to the last day of departure from the camp. All the performers on stage interlocked arms as they thanked Roosevelt.

We send our thanks to Roosevelt
Who heard us beyond the stars,
Who sent an angel to the world
To free us from this farce.

We soon leave Fort Ontario
And try to find our hearth;
To find our life, our work and move
At liberty on earth!

Newly written ending to *The Guilded Cage*

Collections of Fort Ontario State Historic Site, NYSOPRHP.

The first one (November 1944) documents the joy of the refugees at seeing the Statue of Liberty upon arrival at NY Harbor on August 3, 1944. The second cartoon from an August 1945 Ontario Chronicle done by Max Sipser documents their distress one year later at being no closer to achieving freedom than when they first arrived. [Collections of Fort Ontario State Historic Site, NYSOPRHP.]

We all sang, danced, and laughed! Of course, "Who sent an angel to the world to free us from this farce" referred to our Ruth. The Talmud says, "Whoever saves a life, it is as if he saved the entire world." We celebrated Ruth Gruber for saving all of us!

Everyone left the theater and went to the Service Club. We took Sylvia so we, too, could continue the celebration there. I didn't want to miss one minute of the festivities. Shary held our baby and watched smiling as I danced the hora with everyone—refugees and all who came to cover this historic event. As we rang in 1946, a pulse of freedom went through me, and life felt strong and promising. I had confidence that we would adjust and assimilate into American society. We would glow in the joy of knowing we could practice our Judaism openly, all while remembering from where we came.

January 7, 1946

We found out today that many officials from different departments held a meeting to accomplish resettlement plans for all of us. They supposedly had a deadline. I began to really believe we would put this part of our lives behind us.

January 17, 1946

Private agencies sent representatives to help. Government agents and journalists swamped the grounds. As part of the 3,900 immigrants a month, we had to go through the process quickly. Immigration inspectors, border patrolmen, officials of the State, Immigration, and the Public Health Service visited Fort Ontario to help us find housing and jobs.

All Shary and I had to do now was leave the United States, go to Canada, and then we could enter America legally. Before we could leave for Niagara Falls, Ontario, Canada we not only had to finish our alien registration and finger printing, but also every part needed for the immigration process had to be completed.

Then about 100 of the refugees left every other day beginning on January 17, except for the group of Yugoslavs. Since our group was so large and exceeded the quota allotment allowed in one month, it took us about three months for all to attain our visas. Beside Sylvia, twenty-two other babies were allowed in as American citizens because they were born in the camp.

We are so close to starting a new life together. Three busloads of refugees left at 6:00 a.m. every other day. We gathered at the service club around 4:30 a.m. to turn in the necessary requirements to be able to board the bus. We left early so that we could arrive at Niagara Falls early enough to obtain our visas and still have time to return on the same day. They provided coffee and doughnuts before we departed to help calm our nerves from anxiousness and excitement. Shary and I couldn't get over that they even thought to do that. There was a buzz in the air among those getting ready to board. We rode for a couple of hours, until we stopped in Buffalo, New York where we received a warm welcome from the community and a hearty meat lunch at Temple Beth El. Then we took the Rainbow Bridge into the town of Niagara Falls in Ontario, Canada. An American consul by the name of George Graves met us there and gave each individual the long-awaited visa, adorned with a special seal and sash, making everything legal. We returned to the bus and crossed back over the Rainbow Bridge later that day. In total 853 of the 982 refugees entered America, our new home.

Finally, we had a country to belong to, one we could trust, and one we were so proud to call our own. We reached the pot of gold at the end of this rainbow and we knew the land of opportunity we'd dreamt about for so long would treat us well.

Before everyone began departing the camp, Shary, Sylvia, and I enjoyed a few farewell parties held at the service club. We did a circle dance called the Hokey Pokey that we learned in Italy from the British Army. We danced together—staff members, private agency workers, and immigration officials joined all of us! We knew challenging days were ahead, but for now we celebrated news of our freedom.

Chapter 19

About seventy communities in twenty-one different states would welcome us and give us a new beginning. After a year and a half in camp, with little to no freedom, we unexpectedly felt like a flock of geese taking off for an adventure, but not so sure how this journey would go. An internment camp has a bad connotation and although we were scared at first, we didn't realize how good we had it. We didn't really have to worry about anything. Now that we were free, the hardest part would begin. It was overwhelming. Fortunately, the National Refugee Service became the agency responsible for our resettlement and worked closely with the Christian and Catholic committees, as well as other private organizations to assist us in finding a place to live and most importantly to make the adjustments necessary to survive in our new environment. They handled all our travel arrangements for our belongings and us. The organizations recognized that we were put out of our own countries. They understood, it seemed, that we couldn't endure experiencing ostracism in our new community.

Where would we go in this golden land of opportunity? What would we do? Leave the comfort of the camp? Be totally on our own? How will we do this?

The choices were many. The majority of people wanted to stay in New York, specifically New York City. However, with the help of social workers and Jewish organizations, we were exposed to cities all over that were opening their communities to us, offering their help to find jobs, homes, and even interest-free loans.

We spoke with about ten families, our Yugoslav "family," as we tried to reach a decision together and finally decided on Baltimore, Maryland, sight unseen. We were told it was a big city and a good place for those of us with children to raise our families. Also, the word Baltimore ends in the word *moré*, which means "sea" in Serbian. Shary and I had always loved the water. We imagined Baltimore to be the perfect city for us to settle in, picturing a place and a climate resembling Florida. We were surprised to find Baltimore nothing like the beautiful resort by the sea that we thought would warm us all year long, but happy to learn the ocean was a just a three hour drive away.

How different we looked from when we literally got off the boat! If you saw us on the street you would think we looked like any other American. We were dressed in American clothes and now spoke English, with an accent, of course. From our experiences for a year and a half in the camp, as well as from movies, radio shows, and newspapers, we grew and changed to fit into American society. We understood the customs and tastes of this country. We understood the values. The fact that no one in the entire camp got in trouble with the Oswego police showed that even though we had been fighting for survival, none of us left undisciplined. As long as we obeyed the laws, we would have the right to live unrestricted. We were ready.

Jewish organizations placed us in a poor section of Baltimore at the Altamont Hotel. A woman waited at the train station for us and brought us to the hotel. We stayed there until they quickly helped me find my first job as a shoemaker and our first apartment for about $45 a month, along with donated clothing and furniture. I earned about $25 a week. We had a small apartment on the third floor of a building on Callow Avenue in Baltimore City with a tiny kitchen, a room that doubled for a living room and sleeping quarters, and a small bathroom, but somehow we were truly happy.

For five years, I worked during the day, as a shoemaker and tried to learn carpentry, but as hard as I tried, I couldn't do it well enough. Then I supplemented with a factory job for five years while attending night school so I could learn English at a level proficient enough for me to obtain an office job. My goal was to become an accountant again and I knew it would be difficult to do this in America.

My English improved and I managed to hone my bookkeeping and accounting skills. In 1950 a wonderful man, Mr. Schloss, decided to give me a chance and hired me as the bookkeeper for the Baltimore Lumber Company. I continued to work at additional part-time jobs to help us meet expenses since Shary became pregnant with our second child the following year.

We moved to a two-bedroom apartment on Linden Avenue where we lived when Shary gave birth to another girl, Florence Linda on November 1, 1951. Florence was named in memory of her mother, Flora, and Shary loved her very American middle name.

Slowly but surely we made a life with the help of the Associated Jewish Charities of Baltimore. Both of us became citizens and chose to speak to our children only in English. We wanted to become patriotic United States citizens and we wanted our children to be true Americans through and through.

No, it was not exactly as we had hoped, but it would be fine…better than fine. We were with our friends and we would create a new life here, together. At least we had each other. At least we knew in our hearts—*Hitler, you did not win. We did!*

Leon Kabiljo   Shary Kabiljo

Taken after they arrived in Baltimore, Maryland 1946

Sarinka (now Shary) with 22-month-old Sylvia Simcha, February 1946

Naturalization Papers, October 1951

Epilogue

Shary

I stayed home with my children until my youngest daughter was old enough to come home from school by herself. Fortunately, to help with our finances, I was able to get a job with the Baltimore City Enoch Pratt Free Library, working in their bookbinding department, which I did for 18 years. This is where I developed my love for books, which I passed on to my children.

As an accountant, Leon was capable with our own finances. He always managed to save money so we had what we needed and worked multiple jobs to provide the best he could for our family. We proudly purchased our first home in 1956.

Isaac, Leon's brother fought with Tito's Partisans for two years and managed to survive the war. After we finally reconnected, we were saddened to learn that he lost his wife and two children who never left the concentration camp. In trying to make sense of what happened, Leon and his brother Isaac tried to investigate the whereabouts of their family. In December, 1941, they were devastated to learn that their mother and grandmother were imprisoned by the Ustasha in Lobor-Grad concentration camp in northern Croatia. A deserted palace of the Keglevich family, turned concentration camp, housed mostly Serb and Jewish children and women. With the Ustasha in charge, they were, of course, robbed but those unwilling to cooperate were systematically tortured and/or murdered. The younger women were raped. Leon cried thinking of his mother and grandmother exposed to the wrath of this revolutionary group. He couldn't bear it. The tears flowed. He said he felt so helpless and guilty for not insisting that his mother come with us when we left, but I tried to reassure him she was adamant about remaining with her mother. We finally received a letter in the mail dated June 3, 1957 in which two witnesses from their town stated that their mother, "Simha Kabiljo was ultimately sent to Jasenovac concentration camp and never came back." Simha, at the age of 65, and her mother, who was 90 years old, were, "… exterminated on December 29, 1941." Of course, we knew in our hearts that she had been killed, but seeing her named typed on the thin onion-skin paper was the final closure that ripped at our hearts and souls again. Now with all hope lost, we mourned again. It was just like hearing it for the first time.

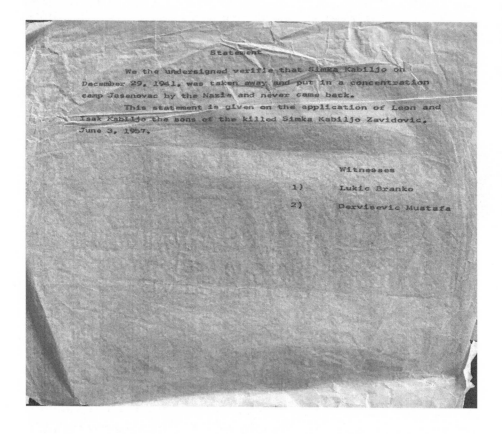

STATEMENT

We undersigned verifie that SIMHA KABILJO the mother of
Leon Kabiljo and his brothers : ELISHA, CEVY, JOSEPH, and ABRAHAM
with their wifes and childeren and his sister Sol with her
husband Joseph and daughter total 25 was taken away and put in
a concentration camp by the Natzis and never came back, as a
resolt of persecution during World War II.

Translated

In 1970, we finally saved enough money and were able to take a long-awaited trip back to Yugoslavia so Leon could visit his only surviving siblings. We first went to Israel and spent time with his only surviving sister, Saphira Papo, who lived near Tel Aviv with her husband Isaac and two sons, Yaakov (who we called by his Yugoslav nickname, Bratzo) and Davo. It had been close to thirty long years, but at last we rejoiced together. Then we continued on to Yugoslavia to visit his brother, Isaac Kabiljo, who lived in Sarajevo with his wife, Vikića (the woman who helped him escape), and their two children Jakića and Silva, same names as his murdered children. They now reside in Vienna, Austria. They had to leave due to the war fought from 1991 to 1999 that led to the ethnic and territorial division of the former Yugoslavia.

My husband, Leon Kabiljo donated one of my father's prayer books to the *United States Holocaust Memorial Museum* in Washington, D.C. This Sephardic siddur (prayer book) measuring five by four inches was published in Vienna in 1890. Inscribed in the book in Hebrew is, *"Hannukah—Nes Gadol Haya Sham,"* along with the English translation,

"A Great Miracle Happened There." In the context of Leon's life, these words took on a personal meaning. It was truly miraculous that this book survived all that Leon had been through, but he kept his promise to my mother that he would do his best to protect this priceless siddur. Along with this book, he donated our circular yellow badge with the Croatian letter Z (Zidov, Jew—used to identify a Jew) that we were forced to wear. We could not part with the tiny prayer book (2.5 by 3.5 inches) from which Leon prayed daily while trying to survive. To this day, it remains in our family's possession.

At the age of ninety-two, my husband told my daughter Linda, who became a reading specialist, that he finally realized why he had been one of the lucky ones who survived. He told her, "One of the reasons I survived was to bring you into this world so that you could help so many children." Unfortunately, he passed away before this book was written, but I was lucky to have been married to the love of my life for sixty amazing years. He died in 2001 at the age of ninety-four, but lives on in our hearts daily.

Now, at the age of ninety-one I am filled with pride knowing how many wonderful lives have come from the two of us and all that they are accomplishing. What more could anyone ask? My Shabbat table is full!

I once heard someone ask a question of Hungarian born Rebbetzin (rabbi's wife) Esther Jungreis (z'l), a survivor of Bergen-Belsen, and a dynamic speaker and author. When asked, "Where was God during the Holocaust?" she shouted back with immense emotion, "You ask, where was God and I ask where was humanity?"

This is a question that needs to be answered whenever humans are selected for annihilation. My hope is people will learn from my story and will not remain silent when Jews or any other innocent groups of people face genocide.

Humanity, although stained, finally showed its face. Because America did not know what to do with us, we lived in an internment camp for a year and a half, but the people of the United States, the government, many Jewish organizations, and Jewish charities saved our lives and helped us begin anew. Humanity showed up outside Camp Ontario in Oswego, which before this episode in history was a little known town in upstate New York. Americans showed up, and I wanted to let everyone know the gratitude that my family and I owe to Ruth Gruber, to the town of Oswego, and to our amazing country.

Thank you, America.

… and thank you for reading my story.

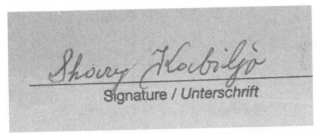

Signature / Unterschrift

Shary Kabiljo (as told to F. Linda Cohen)

Shary on her 90th birthday

Shary Kabiljo, born July 11, 1918, passed away quietly on March 6, 2010, at the age of 92. Both daughters held her hands to her last breath. Unfortunately, she did not live to see this book published, but she confirmed that all she heard was as she remembered it to the best of her ability.

She cherished Ruth Gruber's book *Haven*, and on many occasions said how happy she was that the book was written to document all that she and Leon experienced. I am proud to have had communication with Ruth Gruber and that she at least read my manuscript when I was preparing to publish this book back in 2010. Ruth Gruber died on November 17, 2016, at age 105.

Shortly before Shary passed away she predicted that her granddaughter Jaime would meet someone and marry. Within the month Jaime met her future husband, Jonathan and a few years after Shary passed away, Jaime gave birth to Shary's twin great granddaughters, Eden Leonie and Sasha Marin. They were named after Leon and Shary.

Shary had just told her granddaughter, Jaime, she
was sorry she couldn't be at her wedding.

Linda visiting the camp

Postscript

My entire life I looked at President Franklin Delano Roosevelt as my hero. After all, it was ultimately because of him that my parents were saved. In doing research for this book, however, I learned that President Roosevelt stayed silent about Hitler's actions for about five years before he admitted to and addressed the growing "refugee problem." The one and only attempt made by the United States to help save the refugees, was allowing up to one thousand refugees to reside at Camp Ontario in 1944, before the war ended. I was fortunate enough to attend the 70th reunion and tour the camp in 2014.

The recorded minutes taken in a twenty-nine minute meeting demonstrates that on December 8, 1942, Jewish leaders conveyed to the President the horrors of the Holocaust and he declined to act until 1944. Of course, I am grateful my parents' lives were saved, but sad to learn how many more lives he may have spared. I share this fact with the hope it will serve as a reminder to all of us how genocide can happen during civilized times and even that the leader of the United Sates of America can turn and look the other way.

I felt devastated when I read:

"Mr. President, we also beg to submit details and proofs of the horrible facts. We appeal to you, as head of our government, to do all in your power to bring this to the attention of the world and to do all in your power to make an effort to stop it."—Rabbi Stephen S. Wise December 8, 1942

This was the only meeting President Roosevelt had with Jewish leaders on this subject.

However, with continued research, Dr. Michael Berenbaum, a world-renowned writer, lecturer, and teacher at American Jewish University delivered a lecture maintaining that President Roosevelt's decisions must be put in the political context of the time. He professes, "FDR was the best: Best of his generation in dealing with the Holocaust, the best of his successors in dealing with genocide; but that is no compliment." Dr. Berenbaum concluded that although President Roosevelt was more responsive than any in his generation and it may have been his best, it still wasn't good enough. He concluded that we are fortunate that President Roosevelt was not only worried about getting himself re-elected, but he also made sure America was ready to get into WWII and win. For this, I am, of course, still grateful to President Roosevelt.

Finally, I would be remiss if I didn't also mention the research revealed in a new book, *RESCUE BOARD The Untold Story of America's Efforts to Save the Jews of Europe* by Rebecca Erbelding. Erbelding provides us with detailed research of how the War Refugee Board was created due to public pressure and the ideals of one man, John Pehle, a German American lawyer at the Treasury Department. He is responsible for convincing President Roosevelt of its necessity and became the War Refugee Board's director because he strongly believed the United States should rescue the Jews from the Nazi genocide. America didn't own the problem of the Jews until 1944. The WRB, created in January of that year, broke all the rules to save humanity and it was also directly responsible for locating the camp in Oswego so they could save 982 lives until the war ended. What most don't know, however, is that the WRB worked tirelessly and discreetly to save tens of thousands of lives. Pehle, with the help of Henry Morgenthau, Florence Hodel and others on their team used international alliances to save lives. For example, "Together they tricked the Nazis, forged identity papers, maneuvered food and medicine into concentration camps, recruited spies, leaked news stories, laundered money, negotiated ransoms, and funneled millions of dollars into Europe." In addition, "The

War Refugee Board tried everything in its power to prevent atrocities, provide relief, and rescue potential victims." They froze assets in our enemies' accounts, and consequently fought the war economically before we technically entered after Pearl Harbor, December 7, 1941. This is a huge untold part of history that shows America did more than we knew to aid humanitarian efforts and wouldn't have happened without approval from President Franklin D. Roosevelt. Although, some say the WRB may have been "too little too late, I still feel for their work during a very complicated period in history.

Rebecca Erbelding also makes an astute conclusion. She proclaims that the number of people "saved" really can't be measured. "While murder is definitive—victims can only be killed once—most Holocaust survivors were "saved" many times, sometimes proactively, but often by accident." As she also says, "Many small "rescue" efforts were needed to save one person." This was very true for my parents, especially my father. In essence, the WRB's efforts, however, may have been intangible, but people like my parents were alive in 1945 thanks to their actions. Most importantly, the details in her book provide a respectable model for the future, if God forbid, ever needed.

God needed witnesses, but all too soon, we will mourn the last survivor's death and the responsibility to recount the horrors of the Holocaust will rest with future generations. How scary to realize that Holocaust deniers are already trying to alter historical facts. The vigilance and actions needed to help prevent genocides worldwide rests not only with our future leaders, but also with each of us, so nothing like this ever happens again. We must always remember.

My greatest hope is that Holocaust victims who were not so fortunate should never be forgotten.

Shary Kabiljo (z'l) 1918-2010 and Leon Kabiljo (z'l) 1907-2001

May the memories of Shary and Leon Kabiljo and all the victims of the

Holocaust be for a blessing.

By reading the names of the victims in our family, it will keep their memory alive.

Leon's mother: Simha Kabiljo (65 years old: exterminated on December 29, 1941)

Leon's grandmother: Sultana Kabiljo (90 years old: exterminated on December 29, 1941)

Leon's brothers: (Each brother had 2, 3, or 4 children.)

    Avram Kabiljo, his wife and children

    Elisha Kabiljo, his wife and children

    Josef Kabiljo, his wife Vikića, and their children

    Sevi Kabiljo, his wife and children

Leon's sister: Solčika Kabiljo (married name unknown) her husband and children

Leon's aunts and uncles

Shary's mother: Flora (Bukića) Montiljo (about forty-eight years old)

Shary's grandmother: Sara Musafia

Shary's aunts: Her mother's sister: Luna (Lunchika) Papo, and her husband Buki, and their young daughter Donitza and her other sister, Rachaela, her husband and children. Also, sister Solčika.

Shary's aunts: Her father's sisters: Flora married Pesach and they had a daughter, Sarina, who married Flora's brother, Yaakov. Blanca, Rivka, Esthera, and Sunkala were also sisters of her father.

Shary's uncles: Her father's brothers: Dr. Davo Montiljo (Dentist), Yaakov Montiljo, his wife Sarina and their twin sons.

Forty relatives from Leon's family as well as an unknown number from Sarinka's family—never to be heard from again.

"All that is necessary for the triumph of *evil* is for good men to do nothing."

Edmund Burke

Shary and Leon Kabiljo's Family

S hary and Leon had two daughters, Sylvia Simcha and Florence Linda.

Sylvia Simcha Rothschild and Florence Linda Cohen

Sylvia Rothschild, a self taught artist, worked as an esthetician, assistant teacher, and later began a business called, Companions Are Us to help the elderly. She married Marvin Rudick and had two daughters. In 1986, she married Irvin Rothschild. Sylvia dedicated her life to helping others, much like her namesake. Sylvia passed away suddenly on December 22, 2017. It was a great loss for her family and friends. Marnie, their granddaughter, graduated with a degree in psychology, and then returned to school to achieve her Masters in Science in Pastoral Counseling. Marnie is now a practicing Licensed Clinical Professional Counselor. Marnie married Stephen Kahn and blessed Shary and Leon with a great grandson, Jacob Logan Kahn. Sylvia's younger daughter, Barbara Epperly, married and blessed them with four great grandchildren: Tyler, Dylan, Cortney, and Zoey Epperly. Barbara works as a preschool teacher.

Florence, named for her late grandmother, Flora, was alway called by her middle name, Linda. Shary found it too difficult to call her Florence, since the death of her mother was still too fresh. Linda married her high school sweetheart, Ronald (Rick) S. Cohen who became a podiatrist. Linda and Rick moved to Michigan where he was in practice for almost forty years. Linda attended the University of Maryland, Baltimore County, and became an elementary school teacher. Later she attended Oakland University in Michigan and earned her Masters in Teaching Reading and Language Arts, as well as certifications to teach those with dyslexia. She retired from Detroit Country Day School after fifteen years as a reading specialist. They have three daughters. Lauren, graduated with a degree in art and teaching, is a talented artist, especially in three-dimensional mediums, and currently teaches art at a Jewish day school. She has a daughter, Kinneret Simcha, named after Sylvia Simcha. Dr. Jaime Zadoff (who married attorney, Jonathan Zadoff) is a full-time optometrist at the Detroit VA Medical Center. They have twin daughters, Eden and Sasha. Meredith (who married Rabbi Yonatan Dahlen) works as a family law attorney.

Leon's only surviving sister, Saphira (Kabiljo) Papo died in 1990 in Haifa, Israel.

Leon's only surviving brother, Isaac Kabiljo died in 1992 in Sarajevo, Yugoslavia.

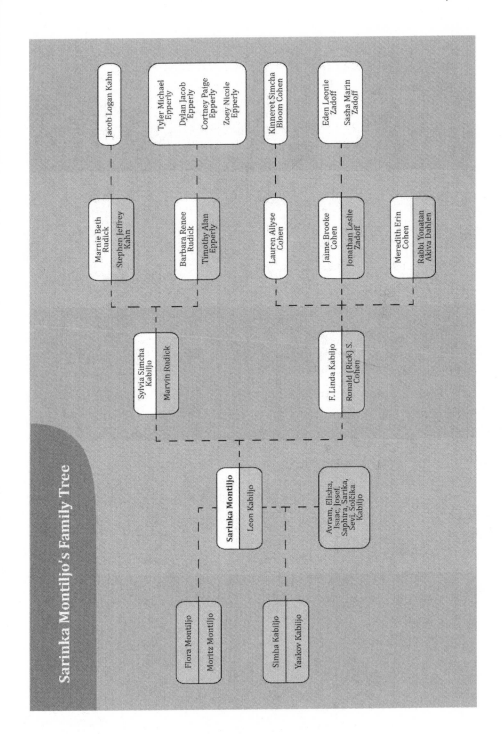

Sarinka Montiljo's Family Tree

The wedding of Shary's granddaughter Meredith to Rabbi Yoni Dahlen, flanked by Linda and Rick, Jaime (sister) with her husband Jonathan Zadoff (on left) and their twin daughters, (Shary's great granddaughters) Sasha and Eden, and Lauren Cohen (sister) on right.

Shary's daughter Linda with her daughter Lauren holding Shary's great granddaughter, Kinneret Simcha

Dylan, Tyler, Tim Epperly, Marvin Rudick, Barbara Epperly, Linda, Marnie, Steve, and Jacob Kahn, Rick Cohen, Cortney Epperly, Lauren Cohen, and Zoey Epperly

Sarinka's Shabbat table would be full!

Glossary

Burek: Pastry of a thin flaky dough usually filled with cheese, spinach, or meat

Cablegram: A telegram sent by undersea cable

Cantor: The Jewish prayer leader also known as a hazzan or chazzan who leads the congregation in melodic prayer, officiates at lifecycle events, teaches, runs synagogue musical programs and offers pastoral care

Ćevapčići (che-vap-chee-chee): Small grilled logs of seasoned ground beef and lamb

Chatan: Bridegroom

Chenik: a member of various irregular Serbian military guerrilla forces that in periods of disorder (as during World War II) resisted Axis invaders and Croatian collaborators who primarily fought (like a civil war) against the Yugoslav communist guerrillas.

Chicken Paprikash: A classic Hungarian chicken dish with a healthy dose of *paprika, giving* this dish its deep brick-red color

Chuppa: Wedding canopy

Davening: Reciting the prescribed liturgical prayers

Demitasse: a small coffee cup

Dobro sam: I'm good.

Dobro veče: Good evening

Doviđenja: Goodbye

Džezva: a small long handled pot with a pouring tip designed specifically to prepare Turkish coffee

Guerrilla warfare: a form of irregular warfare, by usually smaller independent forces in which armed civilians use military tactics including ambushes, sabotage, raids, etc. to fight a larger military

Kako ste: How are you?

Kallah: Bride

Kishkes: Yiddish slang for a person's gut

Kolo: A fast paced folk dance common in various South Slavic regions

Kosher food: Food that follows the dietary laws of Judaism

Kruščica (Krooshchitza): A village near Travnik, in Serbia

Ladino: A created Spanish-Hebrew language that was used by Sephardic Jews wherever they settled.

Mourner's Kaddish: A prayer that is commonly referred to as the "Mourner's Prayer because it is said in honor of the deceased to show that despite the loss, they still praise God

Nonna: Grandmother in Ladino

Orthodox Judaism: The most observant sect of the Jewish people

Partisans: Irregular fighters who participated in the resistance against the Nazis during World War II

Pastel: Savory meat pie

Palaćinka: crepe-like pancakes filled with jam, rolled and sprinkled with powdered sugar

Quonset hut: A temporary, lightweight, semi-circular structure

Rebbetzin: Rabbi's wife

Sephardi Jews: Jewish people who were expelled from Spain in 1492

Shabbat: A 25-hour period in which we refrain from work and feed our spiritual souls

Shehecheyanu: A Hebrew blessing (Hebrew: וניחהש)

Shema: A most reverent prayer recited on one's deathbed, as well as every morning and every night. This prayer is an affirmation of Judaism and a declaration of faith in one God.

Shmata: An old ragged garment.

Siddur: Jewish prayer book

Slivovitz: a plum brandy made in Yugoslavia

Talmud: The collection of ancient rabbinic writings consisting of the Mishnah and the Gemara,

constituting the basis of religious authority in Orthodox Judaism.

Tefillin: A pair of small black leather boxes enclosing inscribed parchment scrolls with biblical verses worn to remind us that it was God who took us out of Egypt. A set includes one for the head and one for the arm.

The National Fascist Party: an Italian political party created by Benito Mussolini as his political expression of fascism. A fascist is a person who is dictatorial or has extreme right wing views.

Torah: The Jewish Holy Bible

Unterseeboot: Undersea boat, more commonly known as the U-boat

Ustaša/Ustaśe: (Also known as Ustashe-plural, Ustashas, and Ustashi): were members of the Ustaša – Croatian Revolutionary Movement, a Croatian fascist,[2] ultranationalist and terrorist organization, active, in its original form, between 1929 and 1945, founded by Ante Pavelić. Its members murdered hundreds of thousands of Serbs, Jews, Roma

(Gypsies) as well as political dissidents in Yugoslavia during World War II.

Valuta: Foreign currency, value of one currency with respect to its exchange rate with another.

Yiddish: A language that incorporated elements of Hebrew, Aramaic, Slavic languages, and Romance languages.

Zaftig: a woman having a full rounded figure, pleasingly plump.

Made in the USA
Lexington, KY
22 February 2019